A
CHRISTMAS
WISH

A
CHRISTMAS
WISH

•

BERNADETTE
PRUITT

AVALON BOOKS
THOMAS BOUREGY AND COMPANY, INC.
401 LAFAYETTE STREET
NEW YORK, NEW YORK 10003

PRINTED IN THE UNITED STATES OF AMERICA
ON ACID-FREE PAPER
BY HADDON CRAFTSMEN, SCRANTON, PENNSYLVANIA

In memory of Buddy and Snuggles

Chapter One

Aunt Margo was made of steel. She could kill a rattle-snake with one shot and get a stalled tractor going in a minute. But at this moment, her bottom lip quivered and her dark eyes brimmed with tears.

"Well, kid," she said, grasping Abby's wrists, "I hate leaving you all alone like this. Are you sure you don't want to go back to Texas with me—at least for a while?"

Abby swallowed the lump in her throat. "No, Aunt Margo. It's not that I'm not grateful for your help in taking care of Dad. You've been wonderful. But I want to stay here in Seattle. I'm going to look for a job, and there's not much demand for English nannies in Bluebonnet, Texas. So please don't worry about me. I'll be fine."

Aunt Margo, her face brown and creased from the Texas sun, smiled dolefully. "Abby Ryan, you're as independent as your old Aunt Margo. But listen to me. This is not England. This is America. You're not only alone, but alone in a strange country. And here in the big city, you can happen onto trouble quicker than you can say 'spot of tea.' "

"I'm no innocent abroad," Abby countered.

The older woman gave her a chiding look. "That's not going to stop me from worrying. We're all that's left of the family. Now that your father is gone, I feel responsible for you. You're the daughter I never had." She quickly wiped away a tear. Her chipped scarlet nail polish looked oddly out of place on her ranch-roughened hands.

Abby studied her aunt through her own tears. Silver-haired and only five-two, she had six feet of presence.

"Aunt Margo, remember what they said about you when Uncle Ed died?" she asked. "They said you were city bred and too soft, that you'd never be able to keep the ranch going."

A twinkle of amusement slowly replaced the sadness in the older woman's eyes. "Now don't be a smarty-pants. I want you to take care of yourself and . . ." There was a knock on the door.

"It's your taxi," a male voice bellowed impatiently.

"Hold on to your socks," Aunt Margo called. "I'll be right there."

Abby gave her a last hug. "Thanks for being so wonderful."

"There will always be a place for you at the Tumbleweed Ranch," Margo said. "Call me if you need the slightest little thing." She picked up an oversize suitcase with little sign of struggle. " 'Bye, sweetie. Be strong."

With a click of the door, she was gone.

Silence fell over the small apartment like a shadow. Abby felt like a dot in the center of a dark and boundless void.

She opened the sliding glass door leading to the balcony. There, before the view of his beloved mountains, was her father's empty chair. She ran her hand over it, and a deep ache coursed through her. The facade of composure that she'd maintained in front of her father and Aunt Margo dissolved. For the first time since his death, the tears flowed freely.

She and her father, a retired U.S. Air Force major, had come to Seattle four months ago. Richard Ryan, though a relatively young fifty, was dying of kidney disease. After being stationed for most of his career at American air bases in England, he wanted to spend his last months in the city of his youth, in the land of his birth. It was the country for which he'd flown into battle, the country for which he had been willing to give his life. He called his last journey home "a return to American roots."

As a young pilot, he'd married Abby's English mother, Grace. England was the birthplace of their only child. But despite Abby's English upbringing, Maj. Ryan claimed she had decidedly American characteristics—independence, ingenuity, and at times, irreverence. He'd always said she was more like his Aunt Margo than her reserved and proper English mother. And although she and her father were close, Abby no more resembled the earnest and intense Maj. Ryan than she did her mother in temperament.

"Why go to the theater when we can stay home with Abby?" her mother once joked.

As a child, Abby had a theatrical bent and enjoyed dressing in costumes. Now, she collected vintage clothing.

When Abby was sixteen, her mother died. Refusing to uproot his daughter at such a time, Maj. Ryan passed up a promotion and signed up for another tour of duty in England. Now, at twenty-four, Abby had also come to love her father's Pacific Northwest with its British-like mist and fishing boats. But her own roots were in England.

The problem was that she couldn't go home, at least not

now. What she didn't tell Aunt Margo was that she was almost broke. Without her father, there was no income. The apartment, with the view she had gotten especially for him, was much more expensive than she had revealed and it had quickly depleted their savings. Her father's bank account had also dwindled considerably due to his illness. Whatever was left, a relatively modest amount, wouldn't be available until his will was probated. In the meantime, the lease on the condominium was expiring in two weeks and, except for the Tumbleweed Ranch, Abby had no place to go.

She stood on the balcony and folded her arms across her chest to insulate herself against the October chill. A mist as fine as gossamer blurred the outline of the Cascade Mountains. With each passing moment, the mist became more palpable, turning from droplets into a driving rain, closing over the view like a curtain. Abby stepped inside, watching the rain from the shelter of the apartment.

During her father's last months, she hated leaving him, even for the shortest periods of time. When they first arrived, he'd been able to get about in a wheelchair. They'd gone to his old childhood haunts—the pier, Pike's Place Market, and even Olympic Park. But as his illness progressed, he lacked the stamina. Under the circumstances, it was almost impossible for her to look for a job. As her father slept, she had made an inquiry at the city's only nanny agency, but she'd been unable to predict when she'd be available for work.

Her father had regarded her choice of a career with wry amusement. "If there's any Brit in you at all, I suppose that's where it is," he'd said. But he reminded her that choosing a nanny school instead of following some of her friends to the university showed some "good, independent American thinking."

She'd spent most of her teenage years baby-sitting for the children of American servicemen. She loved the little ones' freshness and spontaneity, their wonder at the world about them. They were the siblings she never had.

She'd chosen Norland College, a nanny school in Newbury, not far from London. For two years, she attended classes in a Georgian country house set on a rolling green pasture. White sheep and black cattle grazed nearby. After a nine-month probationary post, she earned her diploma. For a year, she cared for the baby daughter of a Swiss attaché, but she was forced to resign when her father's illness worsened.

That she was trained to support herself, however modestly, provided some comfort to the major. "My dear," he'd said, "you've chosen a field that will always be in demand. People will always be having babies."

In the months before his death, she did everything she could to impress him with her efficiency so he wouldn't worry so much about leaving her alone. She paid the bills promptly, prepared meals, and got him to medical appointments on time.

A lump rose in her throat as she thought how courageous he'd been throughout his ordeal. If only she could be half as brave.

The agency was called "Auntie Nanny's" and was in a restored Victorian house. Arriving by taxi, Abby was ten minutes early for her appointment. She wore a gray wool skirt and a black boiled wool jacket for a sensible nanny look. But at the round neckline of her jacket, she wore a splashy scarf of fuschia, black, and turquoise that reminded her of a child gone wild with crayons. It was a concession to her own impulses, which tended to be bold when it came to clothing. From the backseat of the taxi, she caught a glimpse of herself in the rearview mirror. Her straight, glossy, sable brown hair was freshly cut at chin length. Her full mouth bore a touch of lipstick. Her eyes, perhaps her best feature, showed a trace of nervousness in their green depths.

She paid the driver and took a deep breath before getting out. She knew from experience that a nanny didn't just simply work for anyone. There had to be some compatibility between a professional child-minder and the family. After all, the parents were entrusting her with their most precious possessions. They had to share the same child-rearing philosophy. But Abby wasn't sure how much of a perfect match she could afford. She needed a job right away.

Helen Waymeyer, owner of Auntie Nanny's, was delighted with her credentials.

"You're our first from Norland." She was a tall, sixtyish woman with stiffly coifed silver hair. "I've visited there and I was very impressed. But . . ."

Abby's heart, which had begun to race with hope, skipped a beat. "Norland graduates are all quite efficient and professional," she said.

Mrs. Waymeyer responded with a maternal smile. "And they have lovely accents just like yours. I didn't mean to imply anything short of excellence. It's just that the nanny market in the price range that your training would command is a bit slow at the moment. Many of our nannies are grandmothers or mothers whose children are grown. Rather than living in, they go to their own homes in the evenings."

Abby swallowed hard. "I'm willing to negotiate."

"We'll see," Mrs. Waymeyer said, resting her elbows on her desk and leaning forward. "I'll do the best I can.

I'm sure that we can place you with the right family, but it may take a little time."

Abby struggled to conceal her disappointment. This might take more time than she thought. There were interviews to complete and parents to meet. It was a process that couldn't be rushed. She realized now what a different proposition child care was in America. The notion of a nanny such as herself was, well, a bit foreign.

For the next several days, there was no response from Auntie Nanny's. Abby, whose anxiety was rising like a hot-air balloon, called the agency daily, only to be told in Mrs. Waymeyer's apologetic tones that there was nothing yet available.

She placed an ad in the newspaper: *Trained English nanny will provide loving and expert care for your children.* But the telephone failed to ring. Meanwhile, the bills came in along with exit forms from the condominium association. Time was quickly running out, along with her courage.

She went for long walks in the rain, making mental notes of notices for "clerks wanted" on store windows. With her father, Seattle had seemed to be a mist-covered playground, a romantic interplay between city, mountains, and seashore. Now it seemed vast and lonely. She felt disoriented and as out of place as the Space Needle poking through the city's rectangular lines. She'd made up her mind to find temporary work in a store or in a day-care center, when Mrs. Waymeyer called.

Within the hour, Abby was sitting across from her desk.

"What we have here," Mrs. Waymeyer said, "is a widower with two children, a girl, three, and a boy, six. His housekeeper is leaving to care for an ailing daughter. But I must be candid with you, Abby. There are two minuses with this situation: The job is temporary, lasting only a few months. The other is . . .'' She hesitated a moment, and Abby's heart gave an anxious leap. "The father is very . . . choosy. Somewhat difficult, to be honest."

Abby's eyes widened. "Difficult?" At the moment, she wasn't sure what bothered her more, that or the fact that the job was temporary.

"He wants only the best for his children," Mrs. Waymeyer said. "He was pleased with the idea of an English nanny but thinks you're too young. However, I convinced him he should interview you anyway. He's a bit stern, but he seemed to be able to see reason in that regard. Still interested?''

Abby nodded.

"Good," Mrs. Waymeyer said. "His name is Stephen Kraft. He's an architect of some prominence. Make your best presentation. Mr. Kraft will accept no less."

It was nearly dusk when Abby arrived at the Kraft home, a Federalist-style gray stucco house with glossy black shutters. The house and the lawn were meticulous in every detail, from the pots of yellow mums by the door to the gleaming brass mailbox. It seemed to say "a perfectionist lives here."

So he said she was too young, she thought with a prick of annoyance. Stephen A. Kraft sounded like a middle-aged stuffed shirt. His poor children, she thought ruefully. A young, exuberant nanny was probably just what they needed.

As she passed under the branches of an old oak that gracefully framed the house, her heartbeat quickened. She stood on the steps and took three deep breaths to calm her nerves. She smoothed her hair, cleared her throat, and brushed any lint or wrinkles, real or imaginary, from her black wool jacket. She stood as tall as her five feet, six inches would allow, and rang the doorbell.

The heavy red door with a small arched window snapped open almost instantly. Abby, her heart lurching into her throat, stood squarely in front of a backlighted male form. His features were yet unclear. "Mr. Kraft? I'm Abby Ryan."

"Please come in," he said. His baritone voice rang with a brusque formality.

She followed him into the living room where he turned and offered his hand. For a man of his size, his handshake was surprisingly gentle, and in the golden glow of a lamp, it was immediately apparent that Stephen Kraft was not what she had imagined. About six feet tall, with solid, square shoulders, he was a man whom she guessed to be in his mid-thirties. His eyes, a clear and penetrating gray, seemed to see inside her. His chestnut hair glinted with a hint of gold. His jaw was square, and planted in the middle of a stubborn chin was a dimple. Abby was struck by his clean and polished good looks.

He shoved his hands into the pockets of his dark, pleated pants. For a moment, he looked at her as if he were studying a painting, one that didn't entirely please him. "You are quite young," he said.

"But quite mature," she countered.

His expression remained stern. "Please sit down, Miss Ryan."

She felt like a schoolgirl being asked to sit after bungling a recitation. As she took her place on an overstuffed, striped sofa, she kept her chin tilted upward in a stubborn show of dignity.

He sat across from her in a large armchair and crossed

his long legs. He took a folder of papers, which appeared to contain her credentials, from a table and opened it on his lap. Resting his elbows on the arms of his chair, he touched his steepled index fingers to a full bottom lip.

"It's important for me to know everything I can about someone I might entrust with the care of my children," he said. "Your training is impressive, your references speak well of you, but I am the final judge. Please tell me about yourself."

Abby told of her upbringing near assorted military bases, her fondness for long walks in the rain, her two childhood treks to Bluebonnet, and her ride in a fighter jet piloted by her father.

When she had seemingly exhausted every detail, he simply responded with, "Continue."

Abby blinked. "I hardly know what else to say."

"Whatever it is, I will enjoy hearing you say it," he said. "Your accent is cute—very quaint."

Abby bristled over what she saw as his failure to take her seriously. "Mr. Kraft, it's not my intention to be cute. Let me remind you that you are the one with the accent."

A hint of a smile played at the corners of his lips, the first break she had observed in his staid and serious demeanor. "So I am," he said. "My apologies to you and all of England."

"I accept on my behalf, but as for the rest of England, you'll have to take it up with them," she said.

He gave the knot of his dark-green foulard tie a tug and unbuttoned the collar of his white, pinpoint oxford shirt. "I'll start the diplomatic proceedings immediately," he said.

Abby gazed at him warily. Things weren't going well at all and she blamed herself for part of it. Her irreverence was always getting her into trouble. The trouble was that no matter how much she tried, she couldn't be anyone other than herself. Why couldn't adults be as easygoing as children?

Stephen Kraft cleared his throat. A brief but awkward pause followed. "Miss Ryan, please don't misinterpret this question, but it's important for me to know. Is there a man in your life?"

"No," she responded, certain for once that she had given the right answer.

"That's too bad," he said.

She felt a flutter of surprise. "I'm not quite sure what you mean."

"Perhaps it's a bit premature for me to explain," he said, stroking his chin.

Abby tensed. Things were going from bad to worse and there wasn't yet a word about the children. At this point, all seemed lost. Englishmen were at least polite with their insults. Americans were much too direct.

"Mr. Kraft," she said boldly, "I'm too young, my accent is amusing, and I don't have the requisite man in my life. Is there anything else?"

His clear gray eyes locked on hers in a flash of intensity. "You have a bit of spit and sass about you, don't you? Didn't your father believe in discipline?"

Her cheeks burned. "Mr. Kraft, perhaps I should leave," she said, rising to her feet. "This isn't going well."

He rose and touched her shoulder, nudging her back to the sofa. His touch was sure and strong, sending an unwanted rush of warmth through her. "Let's talk about the children."

Relenting, she sat back down. After all, the children deserved a second chance. They needed someone and they couldn't help it if their father was next to impossible.

Stephen Kraft took a long, slow breath and suddenly appeared very tired. A crisp lock of hair fell over his forehead. He studied his large, square hands a moment, then looked up at her. The spontaneity he'd exhibited in the moments before gave way to hesitancy.

"My wife and her parents were killed in a plane crash about a year and a half ago. Daphne is three and doesn't remember much about her mother. Peter is six and he still talks about her. It has been very hard on us, but we're managing." His eyes darkened, his jaw stiffened. A grief yet raw washed over his face, flooding Abby with sympathy. She didn't like the man, but couldn't help but be affected by his sorrow.

"I'm sorry," she said softly.

"Thank you," he said awkwardly. "The first help I had was a young woman. Things didn't work out. After four months, I had to let her go. Then I was fortunate enough to get Mrs. Bybee. We're very compatible and the children love her. The problem is that her daughter is receiving a kidney transplant and she needs several months off to care for her." He stood and thrust his hands in his pockets. He paced nervously across a faded red-and-blue Oriental rug. Then he stopped and faced her. "Let's start with the topic of spanking, since we've already broached the subject of discipline," he said with a wry smile. "How do you feel about it?"

"I don't spank children," she said. "I think withholding privileges is a better way to correct behavior."

"I agree," he said.

Abby felt a thump of surprise.

"What do you consider suitable activities for children?" he asked.

Abby launched into a lengthy explanation of crafts, reading, exercise, and educational activities, with television kept to a minimum. They talked about diet, bedtimes, and household duties. "I should explain that I'm a nanny," Abby said, "and my job description is mostly restricted to the care of children. It doesn't cover heavy cleaning and home maintenance."

"I understand," he said. "Now, let me introduce you to the children."

Abby was struck almost speechless by how quickly things started moving. Before she could get her bearings, Stephen Kraft returned to the living room leading a child by each hand. They both had their father's chestnut hair. The girl sucked her thumb. The boy studied Abby gravely while running a miniature toy car back and forth over his chest.

"Daphne and Peter, I'd like for you to meet Miss Ryan," their father said, giving Peter a gentle nudge. The boy's hand met Abby's in a sticky handshake.

"What nice manners," Abby responded. She reached out and tried to entice the girl to come to her. After a moment of hesitation, Daphne sat shyly next to her.

"Amazing," their father said.

"What's so amazing?" she asked.

"That Daphne would come to you. She doesn't like strangers at all."

Abby laughed softly and gave one of the child's curls a playful flip. "Mr. Kraft, children are like puppies. They have an innate sense of who has a heart for them."

Abby chatted with the children for a few minutes. When

it came time for them to return to the kitchen where Mrs. Bybee was sitting with them, they left with hesitation.

"I would like for you to start as soon as possible," he said as soon as the children left the room.

Abby stood in surprise. "But Mr. Kraft, we haven't discussed salary and . . ."

"I'll pay the top rate," he said. His chin was stubbornly set. "There's nothing else to discuss."

Abby felt a flare of annoyance. "Yes, there is, Mr. Kraft. There's one very important thing. And that's that you and I don't seem to get along."

"Your qualifications are excellent and the children like you. For that, I'm willing to overlook the fact that, well, the chemistry isn't so good between us."

"But a good relationship with a parent is essential," she argued. "I don't like settling for second best."

"I'm afraid you're going to have to, Miss Ryan," he said coolly. "The fact that we don't get along is precisely one of the reasons I'm hiring you."

Chapter Two

Abby arrived at the Kraft house with two suitcases and a stomach filled with butterflies. It was just short of nine o'clock and the sky was a leaden gray, threatening to drop more cold drizzle at any moment.

Stephen Kraft had made arrangements for a taxi to pick her up. As the driver had crested the winding street leading to the two-story house, Abby's anxiety rose. In the two days since they'd met, she'd been haunted by his aloofness. But she had no choice but to take the job. In addition, she sensed that these children needed a cheerful adult in their lives. She didn't doubt that Stephen Kraft loved his children, but there was a lingering sadness about him, a brooding preoccupation. And after all, wasn't she in this business for the children?

Abby rang the doorbell, setting off a merry chime that contrasted oddly with its owner's disposition. Within seconds, a plump, middle-aged woman appeared at the door. Her round cheeks were flushed, her short gray hair in disarray. "You must be Abby," she said, her tone musically maternal. "I'm Mrs. Bybee. Come in, dear."

Abby formally introduced herself and shook the woman's housework-roughened hand. "I'm very pleased to meet you," she said. "Mr. Kraft must be waiting for me."

"I'm sorry, but he isn't here," the older woman said, clasping her hands over an ample bosom. "He's at his office and will be home this evening around six. He asked me to help you settle in."

Abby felt a pang of surprise. She expected more supervision from the discerning Mr. Kraft.

"Peter is in school and Daphne is at her preschool," Mrs. Bybee explained. "She goes two days a week. Let me show you to your room."

Abby lugged her suitcases up a staircase that curved gently from the center hallway. At the end of an upstairs corridor, Mrs. Bybee opened a door. Abby followed her inside and set her luggage down. She gazed around a room painted a soft blue with sparkling white woodwork. Open shutters at the windows revealed a wooded backyard. A squirrel chattered just yards away. The room was small, but tastefully decorated with a multicolored quilt and scrubbed pine furniture. "It's lovely!" she exclaimed.

"Mrs. Kraft loved decorating," Mrs. Bybee said, her tone hushed. "Even though they could afford more expensive things, she made some of the curtains herself and loved finding bargains in secondhand furniture stores. A nice, down-to-earth woman she was, and she was crazy about those children. Such a tragedy," she said, shaking her head.

"How long have you known the Krafts?" Abby ventured.

"I've known her family for years. In fact, I did some housekeeping for them when Diane—that's the children's mother—and her younger sister Kendall were small. Now there's no one left of the family but Kendall. Kendall is still single so she has no family of her own.''

She absently plumped the pillows on Abby's bed. ''I worry about the way Mr. Kraft keeps inside himself.'' She moved toward the door. ''Let me show you the children's rooms.''

Both were across the hall. Peter's was decorated in blue and yellow plaid with pictures of zoo animals on the wall. Daphne's was done in pale yellow. A single shelf holding dolls and other toys wrapped around the room. In each room was an eight-by-ten portrait of a woman with a bright smile and blond, shoulder-length hair. She had a fresh and natural look. ''Their mother,'' Mrs. Bybee explained softly.

''She was very pretty,'' Abby said, feeling another pang of sympathy for the children.

''Sweet, too,'' Mrs. Bybee said, stepping outside the door. ''And at the end of the hall is Mr. Kraft's room. Of course, there's really no reason for me to show it to you.''

By early afternoon, Mrs. Bybee had shown Abby the inner workings of the kitchen with its large pine table, glass-front cabinets, and Dutch tiles. Next to it was a television room overlooking a flagstone patio and small flower garden. She was given a glimpse of Stephen Kraft's study, a dark-paneled room with closed shutters. She could see little except a desk and a drafting table. ''The children are not to go in unless he's there,'' she said, ''so the door should remain closed.''

By the middle of the afternoon, Mrs. Bybee had filled her in on the children's routines, their likes and dislikes, and had given her a tour of the neighborhood, a quiet and hilly enclave thick with trees. The children were collected from school and while Mrs. Bybee prepared supper, the sky cleared long enough for Abby to take the children to a nearby park. When they returned home, a dark-blue Volvo sat in the driveway.

"Daddy's home!" Peter squealed, rushing toward the front door. Daphne, her little legs pumping to keep up, followed.

When Abby entered the house, she found Stephen Kraft in the hallway. Dressed neatly in a gray tweed jacket and a burgundy wool knit tie, he knelt, holding each child close. His eyes were without their customary coolness, the line of his jaw without its hard edge. But at the moment his eyes met hers, they seemed to revert back to their serious gaze.

He stood up and sent the children into the kitchen. "Miss Ryan," he greeted her formally.

"Please call me Abby," she said.

He looked at her wearily. "Whatever happened to British formality?"

"Whatever happened to American informality?" she asked.

He raised an eyebrow. "All right. Abby it is."

For an awkward moment, she waited for him to suggest that she might call him Stephen. It might help thaw the icy air between them. But instead he asked for a report on the children's activities.

"Good," he said, after she gave him the details. "After dinner, after the children are in bed, I'd like to see you in my study."

Abby was grateful for Mrs. Bybee's presence during dinner. But her light chatter over meat loaf and scalloped potatoes wasn't enough to distract Abby from her worries about her relationship with her employer. Why was he so stiff with her, yet so relaxed with Mrs. Bybee? Perhaps that would change when they got to know each other better, she told herself.

The slightest of chinks in his armor appeared while she was bathing Daphne. She was wrapping an imaginary stole of soap bubbles around the child's shoulders when she sensed someone behind her. She turned to find Stephen standing stiffly in the bathroom doorway with his arms folded across his chest. His white shirt was rolled up at the sleeves, his collar open, and his tie knotted loosely.

"Daddy, look," Daphne said, her hair a lather of shampoo. "I'm a fairy princess."

Abby reshaped the wilting lather spikes of her crown and handed the child a small plastic mirror. She squealed in delight.

"We made Peter a beard and called him Rip Van Winkle," Abby said.

Stephen's eyes were guarded.

"Daddy, bubbles are fun," Daphne said. "Let Abby give you a bath."

The washcloth Abby held dropped into the water with a splash. She turned just in time to see a muscle in Stephen's jaw jump. His eyes, initially flintlike, flickered. Then the barest trace of a smile touched his lips.

"That's not covered in Abby's list of duties." His voice was tight.

What did it take to make this man laugh? Abby wondered. What did it take to break through the emotional cocoon in which he had wrapped himself? Impulsively, Abby turned and with her index finger flicked a dollop of suds on Stephen's chin. Daphne giggled.

"There," Abby said, "we've plugged the hole in your daddy's chin."

Recoiling, he gave his chin a quick swipe with his hand

and shot her a look of reproach. "I guess I should consider
myself fortunate that you didn't use quick-drying cement,"
he said wryly, exiting the room.

Abby squeezed her fist to squelch the warm tingle in her
finger from accidentally brushing his bottom lip. And as
her finger had slid down his chin, she'd felt the abrasion
of his beard. It had only been a playful impulse but he'd
left her with the feeling that she had crossed into forbidden
territory. Worse yet, touching him had set off a spark within
her. It made no sense. How could fire ignite from touching
someone whose emotional thermostat was set at zero?

After putting Daphne to bed, she found Stephen Kraft
waiting for her in his study. He looked up impassively from
a sheaf of blueprints and motioned to a leather chair in front
of his desk. "Please sit down."

Abby felt like an errant schoolgirl before the principal.
"Mr. Kraft, I'm quite sorry . . ."

"Let's get down to the business at hand," he said, rolling up the prints and thrusting them into a tube.

Abby's cheeks tingled with reprisal. Thank goodness he
was kind to the children, or she would put him in his place
regardless of the consequences. "Certainly," she said with
compliance.

"As you know," he said, "Mrs. Bybee's daughter is
very ill and she needs to take leave as soon as possible. I
would like for you to assume your full duties tomorrow.
You will be able to reach Mrs. Bybee by telephone if you
have any problems."

Abby nodded.

"I don't like doing this," he continued, "but I have to
go to Canada for two days to work on a project. I'll leave
you with my schedule and telephone numbers where I can
be reached."

As he jotted down information from an appointment book, Abby discreetly studied the room. There were overflowing bookcases along two walls and a tattered Oriental rug on the polished oak floor. On one wall were baby portraits of the children. On another were gold-framed sketches of famous buildings, from the Taj Mahal to St. Basil's Cathedral. But what struck Abby most was the picture in a heavy brass frame on his desk. Barely discernible from the angle at which she was sitting, it was the same picture that had been placed in the children's rooms. It was a portrait of Diane Kraft.

He handed her an itinerary written in a neat, square hand. "I will call tomorrow night," he said. "Kendall, my wife's sister, will be dropping by to see the children sometime tomorrow. I've told her about you. I'm sorry I won't be here to introduce you."

His speech was wooden, as if he were merely going through the motions of his life. "Have the children up by six so I can say good-bye to them," he continued. "I'll drive to the airport, but I'll leave you the keys to the minivan. The tank is full, the oil is fresh, and . . ."

"Keep in mind that Americans drive on the right," Abby finished.

The corners of his mouth turned faintly upward with a mix of amusement and vexation.

"Actually, I was going to say that it's outfitted with a cellular phone."

"That's good," she said. "I'm sure I'll manage quite nicely. Please don't worry."

"I won't," he said.

But the sadness in his eyes told her that when it came to his children, he would never be at ease, because they were all he had left. And although more than a year had passed since his wife's death, Stephen Kraft still grieved.

The next afternoon, Abby sat on the living room sofa with a child on each side. A book on dinosaurs lay open on her lap. She had bought the book just that morning and was reading to them the tale of the earth millions of years ago.

"Were there cowboys then?" Peter asked.

Abby smiled. "Not yet, because there weren't any horses or cows."

"Were there dinosaurs in Seattle?"

"It's possible," she answered. "There have been skeletons found in the western United States. In fact, dinosaurs roamed the entire earth. Some were little and some were very big."

"As big as an elephant?" Daphne asked.

"Bigger," Abby said. "Longer and taller than a house."

The eyes of both children shone with interest. This was one of the things she loved about being a nanny—bringing the excitement of new knowledge. And she felt at home with this subject. It had been an interest of hers since childhood, when her father introduced her to the mysteries of another time and took her to explore museums. The thought of him brought a pang of loss.

"Bigger than a mountain?" Peter asked.

"Not that big," Abby said. But before she could finish, the doorbell rang.

Peter scurried to the window. "It's Aunt Kendall," he announced.

Abby opened the front door to find a blond woman in her late twenties. "You must be Abby," she said, her tone formal. She stepped inside. "I'm Kendall Vanderberg. Stephen's wife was my sister."

"I'm Abby Ryan. I'm pleased to meet you," she said, offering her hand. Kendall responded with a cool, limp grasp.

Kendall entered the living room with an air of familiarity, leaving an aura of delicately scented perfume. She wore a finely tailored blue tweed blazer, a white silk blouse, and fluid navy blue trousers, all elegant in their understatement. Her hair was professionally styled, her makeup subtle but perfect. And she bore a startling resemblance to pictures of her dead sister.

"Hello, dears," she said, giving each child a perfunctory kiss. "How are my little ones?"

"Fine," Peter said. "Look," he said, thrusting the dinosaur book into her hand. "We have a new book."

"Careful, sweetie," she said, inspecting a crimson nail. She buffed it lightly on her sleeve. "Aunt Kendall just came from the manicurist." Gingerly, she opened the book and fanned through a few pages. "Such scary animals, aren't they?" she asked, handing the book back to him.

"Abby says that not all of them were mean. She knows a lot about dinosaurs. You can dig in the dirt and find their bones," he said, his sneakered feet swinging back and forth from the edge of the sofa.

Kendall turned to Abby and smiled. A touch of insincerity played on her glossy lips. "How are you and the children managing?" she asked.

"Very well, thank you," Abby responded. "They're both very good children and we're going to be quite good friends."

As she spoke, Abby could sense that Kendall was making a critical inspection of her. She was suddenly conscious of her baggy gray sweatpants, faded Oxford University sweatshirt, and worn sneakers. Wisps of dark hair had escaped from the ribbon at the back of her neck and were tickling her cheeks. She felt as if she were being evaluated for membership in an exclusive club and failing to make the grade.

"So you're from England, are you?" Kendall asked.

"Yes," she said, pushing back the wayward tendrils from her face.

"I understand the English are big on servants such as you," Kendall said.

Abby's cheeks warmed under Kendall's slightly condescending gaze. "A high value is placed on child care," she explained. "A nanny is considered more on par with a teacher."

"I see." Her tone suggested she wasn't entirely convinced.

Abby felt a tinge of a headache coming on and not all of it had to do with Kendall Vanderberg's expensive fragrance. "Please sit down and let me get you something to drink," she said, thankful that British politeness tended to prevail in even the worst social situations.

"No, thank you, dear," Kendall said. "I was just on my way to the club." She gave the room a sweeping look. "It seems that all is in order here. Have you by chance heard from Stephen since this morning?"

"He is supposed to call the children from Vancouver this evening," Abby said.

"He's such a dear, isn't he?" Kendall tossed her blond locks back.

Abby was momentarily at a loss for words. She found Stephen Kraft much too aloof, much too humorless, to be endearing. But despite her feelings, she answered with a nod.

"Well, in the several months that you're here, I'm sure we'll get to know each other better," Kendall said, untangling a set of gold bangles with a shake of the wrist. She turned to the children who were listening from the sofa, and touched their cheeks. "Tell Daddy that Aunt Kendall sends her love, would you?"

Peter nodded. Then with a quick nod at Abby, Kendall Vanderberg strode out the door, the heels of her finely crafted loafers clicking on the oak floor. Through the curtains a few seconds later, Abby could see the blur of a small red car.

After dinner, during which she introduced the children to fish and chips, Abby took them for a walk around the neighborhood. An after-dinner walk was a healthy habit, she contended, and it helped wind the children down for bed. When they got back to the house, the telephone was ringing. It was their father.

"Where have you been?" he asked, his voice touched with annoyance. "I've been worried."

"You worry too much," Abby said. "Didn't you get the recording?"

"You mean Daphne reciting 'Hickory Dickory Dock'?"

"Sorry, we were just having a little fun. I forgot to set the recorder right again."

She heard a deep sigh at the other end. "How are the children?" he asked anxiously.

"Safe, sound, and happy."

"Do they miss me?" he asked.

"More than I do," she quipped.

In the ensuing silence, she could almost hear the line

crackle between them. "Let me speak to them," he said sternly.

Feeling wickedly lighthearted about their exchange, Abby put Peter on the line. Getting Stephen Kraft mad at least took some of the starchiness out of him. Abby had come to realize that he needed to be kept off center. He was a man who needed to learn to love something besides his work and his children. For the children's sake, he needed to regain his love of life. She was going to help him do that whether he liked it or not.

On the afternoon before he was to return, Abby and the children baked sugar cookies. Peter had said they were his father's favorite. Since it was a few weeks before Thanksgiving, she helped Peter and Daphne make Native American headbands with bird feathers they found in the backyard. She taped a large picture of a turkey that Peter had colored to the refrigerator door. On the mantel, she placed a collection of gourds. She hung an autumn wreath that she had bought with her own money on the front door.

Stephen arrived around nine o'clock, about an hour after the children's bedtime, but Abby allowed them to stay up. She knew they didn't need any coaching to give their father an enthusiastic welcome, but she wanted this welcome to be special. So she told them to wear the headdresses they'd made and to give their father a special greeting. The Kraft house had an air of sadness that needed to be dispelled.

As soon as the lights of the Volvo flashed into the driveway, Peter and Daphne went careening out the front door, their arms open wide. In the dim light, Abby saw Stephen Kraft bend over and lift them off the ground. She stepped back inside the doorway.

"Welcome home, Mr. Kraft," she said as he entered, carrying a child in each arm. Their arms were entwined around his neck. Daphne had lost her feather. Peter held his father's briefcase. Stephen's hair glistened from the mist and his tie was flipped over one shoulder.

He set the children down. "Hello, Abby," he said stiffly.

She experienced a wilting feeling from the lukewarm greeting. "How was your trip?"

"Everything went well. I trust all is well here."

"Fine," she said, somewhat formally. "The children and I have been decorating for Thanksgiving."

His brows furrowed and his bottom lip jutted out, a reaction that left Abby bewildered. He said nothing.

"Daphne and I are Indians," Peter said proudly.

"I can see," he said, his tone flat.

Abby couldn't understand this complicated man. She only wanted to bring some joy into his life and the children's and he refused to let it in. "Let me get you something to drink," she suggested.

"Thank you, but later, maybe," he said. "I'd like to spend a little time with the children. I'll be in my study."

As he passed through the living room, a glance at the gourds on the mantel brought him to an abrupt stop. Then he turned and went inside the study.

A feeling of vague despondency rocked Abby's normally cheerful demeanor. Although he trusted her with his children, the man didn't seem to like her. She didn't deny having a tendency toward impertinence. She, like Aunt Margo, seemed to have been born that way. But she wanted to help snap Stephen Kraft out of his sadness for the sake of his children. She understood grief. She missed her father painfully. Yet she knew that sadness, like happiness, was contagious and that it wasn't good to expose children to too much of it for an extended period of time.

Abby remained in the living room and sat down with a

mystery novel. But she couldn't concentrate. She'd been with the family for a week now. Peter and Daphne had gotten over their initial shyness and were adjusting well to Mrs. Bybee's absence. But Stephen Kraft seemed as impassable as ever.

She realized suddenly that the house had become unusually quiet. There was no children's patter, no voices. She got up and walked to the study and found the door ajar. She looked inside and something inside her stirred. The father and both children were asleep in a large gray leather club chair. Daphne dozed in her father's lap, her tousled curls against his chest. Peter, nestled in the crook of his father's arm, lay with his cheek against his father's shoulder. On Stephen Kraft's lap lay an open storybook.

Abby stood rapt in the doorway, studying the scene. Stephen Kraft's lips were parted slightly. The side light from the adjacent floor lamp deepened the dimple in his chin. His hair fell recklessly over his forehead and his face was shadowed with a day's growth of beard, but Abby had never seen a man with such physical appeal. For an instant she forgot that she was looking at a man who, when awake, was as cool as a coastal rain.

She bit hard on her lower lip to bring herself back to reason, but it was hard to take her eyes off the sleeping family. A quick glance at her watch told her it was ten-thirty. They should all be in bed. Yet somehow, she felt that waking them would be an intrusion. But as soon as she turned to leave the room, she caught Stephen stirring out of the corner of her eye. He squinted at her with sleepy eyes.

She felt the color in her cheeks deepen. "It's ten-thirty, sir. I'll be happy to put the children to bed."

He looked slightly embarrassed. "We can do it to-gether," he said.

Abby took Daphne from his arms. Carrying Peter, he followed her up the stairs. It took only moments to settle them in their beds.

"Good night, Mr. Kraft," she said as he stepped into the hallway. "I know you're very tired."

For a moment, he studied her intently. "Abby, if you don't mind, I'd like to have a little talk with you." Something about his tone was unsettling.

Her stomach clutched slightly. "Certainly. I'll make some tea if you like."

He nodded. "I'll meet you in the study."

Abby made the tea weak so it would be less likely to disturb their sleep. She put the cups on a tray with slices of lemon and a plate of sugar cookies. She carried it into the study where Stephen was sitting in the club chair nervously tapping a rolled magazine against his palm. His mouth was quirked in apparent vexation. Abby's nerves jumped.

She set the tray on a small table between them, sat in a wing chair across from him, and poured the tea. He picked up a cookie and frowned.

"The children said they were your favorite," she said.

He set the cookie back on the plate.

She tensed. "Is something wrong? Is it something about my care of the children?"

He looked at her with haunting directness. "No, Abby. You're doing a fine job with the children. It's something else."

She braced herself for a scolding for her flippancy on the telephone.

He took a sip of tea, then set it down. "I'll be direct,

Abby,'' he said, his eyes piercing. ''Don't make a play for me.''

Her cheeks turned scalding hot. Normally quick with a comeback, Abby was momentarily without a response. ''I'm a professional, Mr. Kraft,'' she said, her voice unsteady. ''How could you think I would?''

He glanced at her warily. ''Kendall said you find me 'endearing.' ''

Her stomach seemed to turn a somersault. ''She said you were a 'dear.' I simply agreed to be agreeable, to be polite.''

His expression softened. ''So you don't consider me endearing?''

Her cheeks tingled. ''I wouldn't have chosen that word.''

A slight sternness still veiled his eyes. ''You've baked my favorite cookies and the house is decorated for the season like my wife used to decorate it.''

She felt a stir of anger. ''I thought it would be nice for the children to give you a good homecoming. I did it for them, Mr. Kraft, and I also decorated the house for them. I understand my duties and responsibilities. My job is to make them happy, to make sure they are safe and well cared for. Any thought that I want to be a nanny to you as well is the product of an arrogant male mind.''

A muscle in his jaw twitched. ''It's the product of a logical mind,'' he countered. ''I'm a widower with two small children. That makes women's hearts melt like ice cream.'' His tone contained a hint of bitterness. ''They see that as a form of vulnerability. A surprising number of women are attracted to that.''

''I didn't realized you'd done a national poll on the subject,'' she said.

He leaned back, steepled his fingers, and looked at her

wryly. There was a glint of amusement in his gaze. "The first person I hired to care for the children was about your age," he said. "She made no secret of her interest in me. It was an unpleasant thing to do, but I had to let her go."

Abby stubbornly raised her chin. "I assure you that I have no such affection toward you," she said. "In fact, there are times, such as this very moment, when I don't even like you. You're stiff, you're aloof, and you have grand illusions about your charms, which incidentally are nonexistent."

A hint of a smile played on his lips, but his gaze remained as penetrating as a laser beam. "Anything else?"

"The only redeeming quality that's apparent to me is that you're a devoted father."

He folded his arms across his chest and tilted his head slightly sideways. "To a nanny, that should be the only thing that matters."

Abby strummed her fingers on her knees. But that wasn't enough for her. Was a little more civility too much to ask for? She was glad that Mother Nature had put so much insolence in such an attractive package, otherwise she might be tempted.

"Let there be no mistake about it," she said. "The children are why I'm here. Everything I do is ultimately for their good. Falling in love with you is not on my list of things to do today, tomorrow, or any time. So don't worry, Mr. Kraft," she said, getting up and planting her hands firmly on her hips. "When I fall in love, it will be with a man, not an iceberg."

Chapter Three

At breakfast, she made cheerful conversation for the children's sake. It wasn't their fault that their father had all the warmth of yesterday's toast.

The curtains were open wide, letting in streams of a rarity—Seattle sunshine in November. She'd picked mums from the garden—yellow, bronze, and purple—and arranged them thickly in a bowl. Bright, lilting opera arias from her own collection played softly in the background.

"An act of contrition?" he asked after the children had been sent upstairs to brush their teeth.

"You could use some sunshine in your life," she said.

He studied her quizzically. He was impeccably dressed in a pale-blue oxford shirt and a geometric print tie. He was scrubbed and shaven and his tawny skin still held a tinge of pink from his morning shower. But his eyes still held that familiar sadness. "Sometimes too much cheerfulness can be annoying."

Abby, purposely wearing a large, frumpy brown bathrobe that she'd guessed Mrs. Bybee had left behind, smiled.

"How curious of you to say that. If I were trying to win your heart, I wouldn't do things to annoy you, would I?"

Without taking his gaze off her he bit into his toast and chewed it slowly. "You're cheeky. Why can't you be nice like Mrs. Bybee?"

Abby felt a little jab of hurt. But before she could respond, the children came scurrying into the kitchen. Abby took Peter's lunchbox off the cabinet and set it on the table. "It's your favorite," she said. "A ham salad sandwich."

She gave him a quick kiss on the crown. "Study hard."

" 'Bye, Abby," he said. The little boy surprised her with a kiss on the cheek.

Stephen Kraft's eyes met hers for a stark moment. She glanced away to avoid their intensity. He rose and lifted Daphne into his arms. "Good-bye, sweetheart. Be good for Abby."

"I will, Daddy," she said.

He kissed his daughter's cheek, a scene Abby had seen repeated numerous times, but it never failed to touch her. Such things *did* make women's hearts melt like ice cream. But he'd forgotten one important thing: She was a trained nanny and nannies didn't let sentiment get the best of them.

At first, it was almost imperceptible, like the brush of leaves against a window or a trickle of water. Then the noise grew slightly louder. It was high-pitched and plaintive. It was a cry.

Abby set down a guide to local children's activities that she had been reading and got up from the kitchen table. "Daphne, do you hear that?"

The little girl sat cross-legged on the floor. She was slipping a purple evening gown on a doll with unnaturally long legs and a wild mane of blond hair. She paused to listen. "Yes. Maybe it's a baby something."

Abby took her by the hand. "Let's go look."

They went out on the patio where the cry became clearer. "I think it's a cat, Daphne."

Abby followed the direction of the sound. Tinged with an edge of desperation, it was now sounding more like a wail. Abby looked among the mums and the shrubbery, then under the maple tree outside the kitchen windows. The animal emitted another cry and Abby looked up. On a branch, several feet overhead, was a gray kitten with luminous golden eyes. They were filled with fear and confusion.

"Oh, the poor kitten," Abby cried, holding up Daphne so she could see. "It's managed to get up in the tree and now it can't get down."

Daphne held her arms upward. "Kitty, kitty, kitty," she called. "Don't be 'fraid. I catch you."

"It needs help, sweetheart," Abby said. "Let's get a ladder."

She lugged a wooden ladder from the garage and positioned it under the tree. "Stand back, Daphne, in case the cat jumps," she warned gently.

After making sure the child was at a safe distance, Abby carefully scaled the ladder. The frightened kitten crouched, then skulked farther down the limb closer to the trunk of the tree. "Don't move, kitty," she pleaded.

The animal meowed loudly as Abby positioned herself on the second-highest rung. She realized then that it was a longer distance to the cat than it appeared from the ground.

She stepped up on the next rung. The ladder shimmied slightly and her heart gave a kick. The kitten was now just a few feet away and huddled in the crook of a limb. Abby took a deep breath and in one deft swoop, scooped the cat in her hand. It let out a cry of ingratitude. On the ground below, Daphne danced a little jig of glee.

Her knees wobbling in relief, Abby, with mewing kitten in hand, glanced at her in amusement. Anxious to place the animal in the child's waiting arms, Abby started to descend the ladder, but in her haste her foot slipped. She emitted a gasp and grabbed the side of the ladder to steady herself, but it was too late. She tumbled six feet to the ground and landed with a sickening thump. Stars flashed before her eyes. Daphne screamed and the cat meowed.

Abby gazed upward, fighting to stay conscious. The tree, which at first seemed to be spinning, came into proper focus. The next thing she saw was Daphne standing over her, clutching the cat to her chest. Suddenly, she became conscious of an intense, pulsing pain in her left wrist. Gritting her teeth, she scrambled to a sitting position and cradled her wrist in her other hand. It was swelling rapidly and taking on a bluish cast.

"Poor Abby," Daphne said. "I get Abby a Band-Aid."

Abby pulled the girl to her in a gesture of reassurance. "I'm afraid a little bandage won't help much. It could be broken. Don't worry, I'll be all right, but I'm going to have to go to the doctor."

The cat struggled in the little girl's arms. "I'll take care of you. I have a doctor kit."

Abby smiled. "That's nice of you to offer."

She rose on wobbly legs. Her wrist throbbed more. Her head pounded. She touched the back of her skull to find a knot. She was in no condition to drive herself to the emergency room. She would have to call the children's father. What would he think of her now?

They put the cat on the screened-in porch with a saucer of milk and Abby telephoned Stephen Kraft.

"What?" he responded, a hint of alarm in his voice.

"I'm afraid my wrist is broken," she explained. "I don't think I should drive to the hospital by myself."

Within twenty minutes, his car appeared in the driveway. Abby, her wrist wrapped in a towel soaked in cold water, watched from the kitchen window. Stephen got out and jogged toward the front door. She met him in the hallway, gingerly cradling her arm.

"Are you all right, Abby?" he asked, his face etched with concern. He left the front door open.

"I think I will be."

"I've called Kendall. She'll be here any moment and she'll look after Daphne." He took a few steps toward her. "Let me have a look."

He gently took her arm in his hands and unwrapped the towel. Abby grimaced. Her wrist was as fat as a sausage.

"Can you move it?" he asked, delicately placing his fingers on it. His touch and the nearness of his face to hers made her heart race. For a moment, she almost forgot the throbbing in her head and in her wrist. Had the fall made her lose her senses?

"It hurts when I try," she finally managed to say.

Daphne eased herself between them. "I'll kiss it and make it all better," she said.

Abby smiled through her pain. She bent over. The little girl planted a wet kiss on her knuckles.

"I feel better already," Abby said.

"Daddy, you kiss it, too," Daphne urged.

Stephen stiffened. Abby's heart seemed to stall in her chest. "One kiss from a little girl is all it takes," Abby said.

"No, Daddy has to do it, too, to make it better faster," she insisted.

He looked at his daughter, then at Abby, and grinned crookedly. He bowed slightly, took her hand in both of his, and placed his lips just above her knuckles. They lingered for an instant. Her veins leaped wildly beneath their heat.

"Well, what do we have here?" a woman's voice inquired crisply.

Abby whirled to find Kendall standing in the doorway, her pale-blue gaze chilly. Stephen gently let go of Abby's hand.

"Daddy was kissing Abby's hand to make it better," Daphne volunteered.

He looked at Abby, then Kendall, with an awkward grin. Abby's cheeks tingled.

"Then maybe you don't need to go to the hospital after all," Kendall said, feigning a smile.

"We should," he responded, "just to make sure all my healing powers are still intact. I appreciate your coming over on such short notice."

"The Society League bazaar committee was very understanding."

He gave his daughter a quick kiss. "We'll have Abby fixed up like new."

He steered Abby gently toward the car. The touch of his hand on the small of her back sent a curious rush of warmth through her. She had almost succeeded in dismissing the feeling until he settled her carefully into the deep leather seat. When he pulled her seat belt over her and fastened it, the unwanted ripple of awareness returned.

"You would make a good nanny," she said.

He smiled one of his rare smiles. "You're talking to a

man who has scorched formula and used a tea towel for a diaper. I'm not without an appreciation for your skills."

She was momentarily taken aback by his remark. She was expecting a scolding for injuring herself. Instead he was giving her a compliment. "Thank you, Mr. Kraft," was all she could say.

He drove with speed and sureness. "Abby, I wish you'd called the fire department instead of risking life and limb," he said, breaking a long silence.

"But it seemed like such a simple matter," she said. "And it would have been if I hadn't been in such a hurry to get down off the ladder."

He cast her a chiding look. She touched her aching arm protectively. She felt a bit foolish. She was afraid that he thought that having her around the house was like having a third child.

He stayed with her during the initial doctor's examination and stood in the shadows while her arm was X-rayed. Moments later, the doctor, a red-haired, freckled intern who appeared to be barely out of adolescence, announced that there was no fracture, only a severe sprain. He wrapped her wrist in an elastic bandage, prescribed cold compresses, and sent her on her way.

"Does it still hurt?" Stephen asked, helping her into the car.

"Not between throbs."

"I think I should get someone to come in and help you for a few days," he said, driving away from the hospital.

"That won't be necessary at all," she protested.

"Will you promise me then that you will take it easy, stay out of trees, and refrain from other daring acts?"

"Only until my wrist is healed."

He cast her a look of consternation. Then there was a lengthy lull between them.

"I'm glad Kendall could come on such short notice," Abby said, breaking the silence.

"My wife had always specified that she wanted her family involved in raising the children if anything happened to her," he said. "Kendall is very busy. She's involved in a lot of fund-raising events, but she's always there when I need her. Because of Diane's wishes, I keep her as involved in the children's lives as possible."

The discussion of Kendall unsettled her. The kindness the woman apparently showed Stephen didn't extend to Abby.

"What about your own family?" she asked.

"There is none," he said. "My father died when I was very young and I was an only child. My mother died before Peter was born. She was an art teacher and her influence led to my being an architect. She loved old houses and liked sketching them. During the summers, we went to towns throughout the Northwest looking for houses to draw. She was a wonderful woman, very strong."

His rich voice stirred something inside her. She found herself stealing glances at his clean profile. But she turned away, telling herself she had no right to such thoughts.

"Diane was somewhat like her," he continued. "Even though she came from a wealthy family, she was making her living as a social worker when I met her. She took pride in making it on her own." His voice took on a raw edge. "I feel very badly that my children had their mother for such a short time."

A little ache coursed through Abby's heart. "It's very sad," she replied, "but they're normal children. They seem to be adjusting well."

He pulled into the driveway. "Yes," he said, "I'm thankful for that. But no child should be without a mother for long."

She experienced a vague sense of alarm. Stephen Kraft, she felt sure, was still grieving for his wife. Would he marry again just to give his children a mother?

Peter burst through the front door just as they were getting out of the car. Daphne followed, the kitten barely visible in her cradled arms.

"Abby, can I sign your cast?" Peter asked breathlessly.

"It's only a sprain, dear. There's no cast, just a bandage."

He looked disappointed.

Stephen Kraft bent over and inspected the kitten at close range. "So you're the little guy who caused all this trouble," he said, stroking his head.

"His name is Boom," the little girl said. "He made Abby fall down and go boom."

"That was my idea," Peter said proudly, his hair mussed.

The father flashed Abby a questioning look. "The cat?"

"It's quite all right with me if the children want a pet," she said.

He stroked his chin contemplatively. "We'd better run an ad in the paper to make sure the kitten isn't someone else's."

The children's faces clouded.

"It's only fair," their father said. "It's very unlikely he has a home—if he is indeed a he—but if no one claims him, he's yours."

As Daphne jumped up and squealed, the cat leaped out of her arms and scurried across the sidewalk. Kendall, who had just appeared in the doorway, recoiled. The children went after the animal, chasing him around the side of the house.

"Is everything all right?" Kendall asked, glancing at Abby's wrist.

"Abby's going to be fine. It was just a nasty sprain, that's all," Stephen said.

Kendall smiled at him sweetly. Then she turned to Abby. "Don't hesitate to call me if I can be of any help," she said. "Stephen knows I'll always be there for him or the children."

Kendall's friendliness toward her seemed to increase in Stephen's presence, Abby noted ruefully. "Thank you," she said. "I do hope that everything went well with the children."

"We get along wonderfully," Kendall said. "I picked Peter up from school, then they got out their crayons after the cat fell asleep."

"We always draw in the afternoons," Abby said. "I rather think that routines give children a sense of security."

They went inside to the kitchen where the children were pouring the cat another saucer of milk. Their artwork was spread over the kitchen table. Abby felt gratified that they enjoyed their regular activities enough that they continued them in her absence.

"Aren't they creative?" Kendall asked, plucking a picture off the table and handing it to Stephen. It was Peter's rendition of Kendall standing by her red sports car. She had taxicab-yellow hair and marine-blue eyes. Under it, he'd written *Ant Kendel.*

Stephen chuckled softly and ruffled his son's hair. "Very good, son."

The child smiled proudly. "Here, Aunt Kendall," he said, taking it from his father's hand. "This is for you."

"Take this, too," Daphne chimed in, not to be outdone. She thrust a scribbly picture of the cat at her.

"You two are darling," Kendall gushed. "I will take special care of these." She turned to Stephen. "I really should run," she said. "I need to check up on my committee meeting."

"Thanks for being available on a moment's notice," he said.

"Always," she replied sweetly. And in one swift and unexpected move, she kissed him. It was no perfunctory kiss on the cheek, but a quick yet delicate brush of her lips tantalizingly close to his mouth.

Abby felt a kick of surprise mixed with alarm. A quick glance at Stephen's face showed the familiar sadness in his eyes mixed with surprise.

Kendall turned to Abby. "Take good care of your arm."

"I . . . Yes, of course," she stammered.

Kendall grabbed her expensive leather handbag from the kitchen counter. She picked up the drawings, then waved good-bye to the children. "I'll see myself out," she said, looking at Stephen, who was now holding the cat.

"Let's get our coats," he said to the children after Kendall had disappeared into the living room. "We need to get Boom some cat food."

As they scurried to the hall closet, Abby watched from the kitchen window as Kendall walked briskly to her car. She unlocked the door, but before getting inside, she folded the drawings in half and tossed them onto the backseat. Abby felt a swell of dismay that made her wrist start throbbing again.

Stephen suddenly stuck his head in the kitchen door. "We won't be gone long," he said. "Rest. That's an order. I'll bring some Chinese carryout."

But she couldn't rest. As she sat in the TV room watching the kitten play with a ball of yarn, the events of the day closed in on her. Stephen's generous show of consideration for her after her injury had altered her opinion of him. The cool exterior had given way to a softer side of him. Despite his attractiveness, he'd been no threat to her emotions because of his aloofness. Now she found the man almost likable, and that unsettled her. She was also concerned about her growing attachment to Peter and Daphne. Mrs. Bybee would be back in two more months and she would have to say good-bye to them. But as a nanny, she was going to have to learn to get used to it. Weren't the English known for keeping a stiff upper lip?

The sound of the front door opening and the patter of children's footsteps startled her out of her thoughts. She went to the kitchen where Stephen was carrying a litter box and a bag of cat food. Behind him were Peter and Daphne, loaded with carryout cartons. They barely set them down before making a beeline to the kitten.

"I wish I'd thought of a pet earlier," Stephen said. "Thanks for rescuing him. The children haven't been this excited about something in a long time."

"I think it was worth a sprained wrist," Abby said with a smile.

He touched her arm lightly, causing her pulse to jump. "How is it?"

"Much better," she said, not adding that it still occasionally ached.

"Good. I'll come home early for the next few days and help you with supper. I'll bathe the children and do whatever physical work needs to be done."

Her eyes widened. His continuing show of consideration heartened her.

"Abby," he continued, "on Saturday evening I'll be going out. It's . . . well . . . dinner and dancing. You'll be able to manage all right by then, won't you?"

Her stomach flipped in surprise. Was there finally a woman in Stephen Kraft's life? "Yes, I'll be fine," she managed to say after a short but awkward pause.

"I should be home by midnight. I'll leave you telephone numbers where I can be reached," he said. "I'll be with Kendall."

Chapter Four

Abby bent over and picked up the kitten's dish to hide the flush of dismay tingling on her cheeks. As Stephen left the room, she busied herself at the sink, giving the bowl several unneeded rinses. *Stop being silly,* she told herself. *Be happy that he finally wants to embrace life again.* Yet the knot in her stomach failed to loosen.

Perhaps if it weren't Kendall, she wouldn't feel oddly uneasy, she mused. If it were someone else, she might be even happy about it, she tried to convince herself. She took a deep breath and vowed to keep her thoughts strictly where they belonged—on the children.

But she couldn't. Throughout their supper of cashew chicken, sweet-and-sour pork, and Hunan beef, she admired his gentle way with the children as he coaxed them into finishing their milk. Somewhere was just the right woman for Stephen Kraft. But that woman wasn't Kendall Vanderberg.

"Peter, Daphne, I have a special announcement." Stephen leaned forward, his elbows resting on the table.

"I know," Peter said. There was an arc of milk above his upper lip. "Next Thursday is my birthday. I'm going to be seven."

"I'm this many," Daphne interjected, holding three pudgy fingers up to Abby.

Stephen smiled. "That's important news as well, Peter, but I have something else to tell you. Saturday night, I'm taking Aunt Kendall to dinner. I want to show appreciation for some of the nice things she has done for us. I won't be gone terribly long, but you will be asleep by the time I come home."

Abby's heart gave a little flutter that she tried to ignore. "We'll make some popcorn and watch a movie," she said, injecting cheer into her voice.

"Okay." Peter nodded with enthusiasm.

"And Boom can have some popcorn, too," Daphne added.

Stephen glanced at Abby, his eyes filled with mirth. Abby smiled, then quickly shifted her gaze to the children. Looking into his clear gray eyes was too dangerous.

The next morning, Abby, wearing Mrs. Bybee's tattered old robe, made her way gingerly down the stairs, holding her bandaged arm. She'd spent half the night reminding herself that she was a woman, not a schoolgirl. That meant that she should be grown up enough to accept the fact that Stephen Kraft was entitled to spend time with anyone of his choosing, even if she happened to be Kendall. After all, she was the children's aunt and no doubt had many good qualities. It was as logical as arithmetic. But for every point she scored in logic, there was a little twinge in her heart.

Padding barefoot across the old Persian rug in the living room, Abby gave her wrist a critical inspection. She'd been instructed not to remove the elastic bandage, but it was apparent the bruising was extensive. A tinge of blue had crept to her swollen knuckles. She wriggled her fingers to keep them flexible. She was certainly fit enough to prepare a simple breakfast of cereal, toast, and orange juice for the Krafts.

Suddenly, she became aware of the aroma of bacon frying. With quickened steps, she entered the kitchen and found Stephen standing at the restaurant-style range. Her heart thumped in surprise. He wore a heavy white terrycloth bathrobe, blue flannel pajamas, and heavy cotton socks.

He greeted her with a barely perceptible smile that was almost shy. "Just helping out a bit," he said, with a fork poised over the cast-iron skillet. His smooth baritone contained its familiar hint of formality. "Hope I'm not making too big of a mess."

"Not at all," she responded, ignoring the flour that dusted the countertop and the black-and-white tiled floor. A small puddle of milk lay next to a bowl of what appeared to be pancake batter. "It's very nice of you, but you needn't have bothered."

"It's nothing," he said with a shrug. He lay down the fork, letting the bacon grease drip on the stove. "How's your wrist today?"

Abby held out her bandaged hand and wriggled her fingers. He placed his palm gently under it, cradling her hand. Her pulse quickened and she pulled her arm away. "It's healing," she said.

But it wasn't her wrist she was thinking of. She was ever mindful of Stephen's boyishly tousled hair and his unshaven face. The stubble across his cheeks and chin emphasized the sensuous curve of his bottom lip and added light to his eyes. Their color reminded her of a clear mountain stream.

"It's said that time heals all wounds." His tone was a bit tentative.

She sensed that he was reminded of his own wound—grief—and she quickly moved to charge the air with a little cheer.

"Let me help you," she said, making her voice light. She reached for the fork, but he was quicker and her hand accidentally closed over his. She jerked it away as if she'd touched a hot stove.

His eyes widened. Abby saw in them surprise and something imperceptible. "Let's not fight over kitchen rights," he said. "For a few days, I'm going to help you whether you like it or not. What I would like for you to do now," he said firmly, pointing to the pine table at the end of the kitchen, "is to sit down until it's time to wake the children. It won't hurt to put your English sense of duty to rest for a while."

Chastened, Abby sat and watched silently as he took the limp bacon from the skillet. It didn't appear to be quite done but she resisted the urge to speak up. "You are really very nice to help," she said. "You must have gotten up at five-thirty."

He glanced at her wryly. "I know you well enough to know that you would be down here at six, sprained wrist or not. This was the only way I knew to keep you from pushing yourself too hard. And don't get the idea that I'm out to show you that I can be a nice guy. I happen to *like* getting up at the crack of dawn, and I was in the mood for pancakes."

"I'm touched by your altruism," she said dryly.

"As you should be," he said, glancing at her over his

shoulder, his eyes filled with mirth. He rummaged in the cabinet for a few seconds, pulled out a griddle, and inexpertly laid it over two burners.

Abby couldn't help but watch his movements and admire the lines of his body. From his shoulders to the gentle narrowing at the waist, he was in perfect form. She suddenly caught herself and turned toward the French doors at the end of the kitchen in search of a distraction. Dawn was just breaking, and a hint of pink played through the leaves of the trees.

"Do you know what I think?"

She turned to find Stephen standing before her, his arms folded across his chest. "I'm not sure I want to," she quipped.

His mouth quirked. "I think you ought to get yourself a new robe."

Abby's cheeks tingled. "What's wrong with this one?" she asked defensively, pulling it tightly around her.

A flicker of amusement danced in his eyes. "I happen to know that that one is a discard of Mrs. Bybee's. She said she was going to make cleaning rags out of it."

Abby stroked the worn brown chenille on her sleeve and a secret satisfaction flooded through her. A man certainly couldn't get the wrong idea about a woman wearing the world's most unprovocative bathrobe. "I rather like it," she said stubbornly. "It's quite cozy."

Stephen shrugged. "Suit yourself, then."

"What did you have in mind?" she ventured.

His eyes danced over the yards of limp folds shrouding her. "Something not so . . . well, big and brown."

"Such as . . ."

Stephen sighed deeply. "Well, I don't know," he said, throwing his hands out in exasperation.

"Well, while you're thinking of some haute couture masterpiece, I'll wake the children."

She traipsed quickly up the stairs, her heart beating rapidly, not just from the exercise but from being in Stephen's presence in an almost intimate setting. It was barely dawn and they were barely dressed. She almost wished he weren't being so kind to her. That made him all that much harder to ignore. And why did he have to look so vulnerable? At this moment, she was almost grateful that he had an interest in another woman.

She roused the children and watched as they washed their faces. At Abby's request, Peter helped Daphne dress, fastening the latches on her red overalls. "I have a surprise for you," she said. "Your father is making breakfast this morning—pancakes."

"Oh, boy!" Peter said, and in an instant, the children were halfway down the stairs.

Abby followed to find them already seated at the table. Stephen was in front of the grill, which was smoking. He looked slightly sheepish. "My test pancake was rather dark."

"It was black," Peter announced.

Stephen winced.

Abby smiled. "Please let me help," she said, reaching over and turning down the heat. Her breath caught as her arm grazed his. She didn't dare look at him.

"I'm here to help you," he said sternly. "Sit down."

She swallowed hard. His tone reminded her of the terse conversations in his study. She knew not to question him. She sat with the children and talked about the birds at the feeder that she'd hung outside the French doors. Within a few moments, Stephen placed before the children plates of misshapen pancakes and soggy bacon. Peter examined his breakfast, then looked at Abby. As Stephen turned away, she quickly put a finger to her lips. "It's very thoughtful of your father to do this," she said. She placed a pat of butter on each top pancake and sparingly added maple syrup. She was relieved to see them eat without complaint.

Stephen added two more plates to the table and sat beside her. "I'll come home early this afternoon," he said matter-of-factly. "I'll pick up Peter from school and run some errands. Saturday, we can take them for a walk on the beach."

There was a murmur of consent from the children.

"That would be lovely," she said, glancing at him for the barest of moments. But it was long enough to bring about a slight surge in her pulse. It was followed by a flicker of anger. It only she could make her heart obey her mind. Distractedly, she poured syrup on her pancakes and cut a small wedge. They were slightly doughy, but edible. "I've forgotten how nice it is to have someone else make breakfast," she said.

"After eating my cooking, you might better appreciate your own," he said, popping a last bite of bacon into his mouth.

"The results were better than *my* first try," Abby replied.

"This wasn't my first try."

Her cheeks warmed.

On Saturday morning, Abby awoke with a vague sense of something being wrong and it was then that she realized that this was the day that Stephen was to take Kendall out. She took three deep breaths and vowed not to dwell on it. She pulled on a pair of black leggings, a turtleneck, and an oversize white fisherman's sweater, picked up secondhand in an Irish fishing village. The sweater, with its heavy cable stitching, came halfway to her knees, and was just old enough and just thin enough at the elbows to have a little character. It seemed quite right for a walk on the beach.

The clouds hung low and gray over the frothing Pacific tide. It was a typical autumn day in the Northwest, chilly and pewter colored.

Abby, with her hands encircling her knees, sat on a blanket and watched Stephen help the children build a sand castle. Earlier, she'd walked alongside him as he carried Daphne on his shoulders, her short curls bouncing. Peter skipped ahead, dragging a stick through the sand. But she later stepped into the background so Stephen could have time alone with them. It was also a way of keeping her distance from him.

She studied them as they huddled over their creation, their chestnut hair blowing in the wind. Suddenly, Stephen turned and came toward her. Sand covered the knees of his gray corduroy pants and dusted the front of his blue sweater. He sat beside her. "It's hypnotic, isn't it? The sea."

She nodded, noting that his pale eyes seemed to match the grayness of the water.

"I have to remind myself that I can't build every castle for them," he said, looking out toward the children. "I have to step away and let them do things for themselves."

"That's the best way," she responded, her tone guardedly professional.

He took a deep breath, his eyes remaining locked on the children. He was so close, she could almost feel the heat of his body. "When Diane died, I was overwhelmed at the prospect of raising two young children alone. Daphne was still a baby. But somehow, I've managed."

"You're doing a fine job, Mr. Kraft," she said reassuringly.

He glanced at her, his gaze softening. "Thank you, Abby."

A brief silence followed. "I feel you should know what happened," he continued. "Diane and her parents were on their way to a resort in Mexico. It was February. The winter was especially bad that year and she'd had a series of colds. Her parents were going for the sunshine and . . ." His voice trailed off. He sighed deeply. "Ralph Vanderberg had been flying for thirty years. An engine problem developed in midair. He tried to make an emergency landing, but he couldn't.

"The Vanderbergs were doting grandparents, but they were careful not to spoil the children. Diane saw to that. She was insistent that we draw up wills specifying that they be the children's legal guardians should anything happen to us. Kendall was to be the guardian in the event she was the sole survivor of the family. Diane had strong family ties and since I have few relatives except an aunt and uncle, that was the most logical arrangement.

"Kendall has been a great help. She helped me find Mrs. Bybee. She has always been here at a moment's notice when I needed her. She's five years younger than Diane was but she has grown up a lot in the last eighteen months. We've leaned on each other, but I feel she has done more for me than I have for her. Needless to say, I feel very indebted to her."

Abby offered a nod of understanding, but her heart felt oddly heavy.

"Look, Daddy!" Peter called. "Look, Abby!" He stood beside a barrel-shaped mound of sand with a leaning turret. The facade was encrusted with seashells.

"I helped!" Daphne added.

"I'm impressed," Stephen said.

Peter picked up a pail and shovel. "Now I'm going to dig for dinosaur bones."

"Me, too!" Daphne said, tearing after him.

"There's a case of big brother worship," Stephen said, looking at them fondly. "Diane had hoped they would be close."

An awkward silence fell between them again. Abby realized once more how deep his loneliness must be, deep enough to be drawn to a woman whose resemblance to Diane Kraft was striking.

"Speaking of Peter," Abby said, trying to sound cheerful, "do you have any special plans for his birthday?"

Stephen stroked his chin. "Perhaps just a small family celebration."

"Why not something involving the neighborhood children as well?" She looked up to make sure the children were outside of earshot. "I could make it a surprise. Let me call in a magician or a clown."

He turned to her. There was something so intense in his gaze that it made her heart jump. "You would do that?"

"Of course," she replied. "That's what nannies are for. And even if it weren't part of my job, I would want to."

"Abby," he said, "I don't know what I'd do without you."

Abby responded with a bittersweet smile. Abby had been trained not to grow too attached to families, but this one tugged at her heartstrings. She'd always remember Stephen Kraft and his endearing children. But would they remember her?

* * *

Abby spent the rest of the afternoon in a quaint shopping area she'd spotted while she was living with her father. It was an odd side street with cottages converted into shops. Stephen had dropped her off while he took the children to the library. He'd apologized that because of his date with Kendall, she wouldn't have more time to herself. He'd make it up to her, he'd said, reminding her that her weekends, for the most part, would be free.

But as she browsed through a vintage clothing shop, her freedom was not the luxury she had anticipated. Without the children, she felt oddly alone. She even missed Boom, who, because no one had answered the ad, was now officially their cat. The gray skies and lapping waves of the Seattle shoreline had reminded her of England. And that stirred in her a vague sense of being lost between two continents.

But she knew deep down that it was not geography that was at the root of her unrest. It was her growing attraction toward a man who was off-limits.

There, she'd admitted it. Admitting the problem was the first step to the solution. And the solution to this problem would be time and distance.

Abby emitted a long sigh and fought to push him from her mind. She had to maintain a demeanor of reasonable detachment, and she had to do it for two more months.

She studied with interest a rack of Forties-era suits with their shoulder pads and peplums. She discovered Capri pants and a Sixties-era hip-hugger miniskirt. She didn't have much of a collection of old American clothing and she resolved to buy some to take back to England. After browsing for a half hour, she selected a long-sleeved black tent dress that stopped several inches short of her knees. It had a decidedly bohemian look that appealed to her. Afterward, she treated herself to a cappuccino in a stand-up bar. Both purchases cheered her somewhat and she resolved to greet the rest of the evening with as many smiles as she could muster.

Stephen picked her up soon afterward. The children had picked up a half dozen books apiece from the library. Peter's were about dinosaurs. Daphne's taste ran toward stories of baby animals. Stephen had a book on the log cabins of Finland and a manual on how to care for cats. He handed the latter to Abby as they drove home.

"And what do you have, may we ask?" He glanced at the bag at her feet.

"A dress," she answered succinctly.

He cocked an eyebrow. "An understatement, I'm sure. What decade will it be this week?"

She shot him a look of annoyance. Yet she was somewhat relieved. He was much easier to deal with when he was being testy. "The turbulent one," she answered cryptically.

"Which one hasn't been?" he asked. "As Mrs. Bybee is fond of saying, life is one thing after another."

"Let me see, Abby, please," Daphne begged.

She pulled the dress out of the bag as Stephen parked in the driveway. "It's a tent dress, sweetheart," she said, holding the black garment up for inspection. "It was the style in the Sixties, thirty years ago. It's old."

"Daddy's thirty-four," Peter announced.

A look of mild chagrin spread over Stephen's face. Then his eyes turned to the dress. "It's short," he observed. "It's . . . nice."

Abby wasn't sure to what she could attribute his relatively good spirits unless it was his impending evening with Kendall. As she busied herself getting a meal of macaroni and cheese for the children, Stephen went upstairs. A half hour later, when she had them settled at the table, he appeared in the kitchen. She was so startled by his striking appearance that she almost dropped her fork. He wore a dark-gray double-breasted suit, a crisp, white shirt, and a black-and-white foulard tie neatly dimpled at the knot. The dark tones brought out the gold in his hair. She turned toward the children once she realized she'd been staring at him.

"I should be home around midnight," he said.

Abby nodded.

Stephen bent over and kissed each child on the crown. "Be good for Abby. I'll see you in the morning."

The children called out their good-byes. A few moments later, Abby heard the snap of the front door. It was a milestone for him, she knew, to be able to go out with a woman for the first time since his wife's death. She then sensed what it must be like for a mother who watches her child ride away on a bicycle for the first time. She was pleased, yet afraid.

Abby and the children spent the evening watching *The Wizard of Oz*. Boom lay curled on the sofa between Daphne and Peter. Abby sat nearby in a plump slipcovered chair as the Tin Man sang, "If I Only Had a Heart." The children, with bowls of popcorn in their laps, watched with rapt attention. But Abby was restless despite her long-standing affection for the old film.

After the movie, she put the children to bed, then went back downstairs to watch television. Not wanting to be alone with her thoughts, she watched *Dr. Zhivago*. But at the end, she somewhat regretted having seen it. After all, it was about a love affair that wasn't meant to be.

She tried to brighten her mood by thumbing through

travel magazines. Sitting cross-legged in her chair, she began reading an article on Westminster Abby.

The next thing she knew, Stephen's hand was on her
arm. "Abby," he said gently, kneeling beside her, "I'm
home."

Her eyes fluttered open and the angles of his face came
into focus. She straightened in a blur of embarrassed in-
coherence. "I'm sorry," she said. "I must have fallen
asleep."

"Not must have, did," he replied. "It's almost one
o'clock in the morning. I'm a little later than I anticipated.
Come on," he said, reaching for her arm. "You should be
in bed."

Suddenly she became aware of a prickling sensation in
her legs. She tried to get up, but the sensation escalated to
such a tingling numbness that it felt like her veins were
filled with needles. She sank back into the chair. "My legs
are asleep," she said with a wince.

"Here, I'll help you," he said, placing a hand on her
bandaged arm. "Sorry," he said, apparently realizing his
mistake. He took her other arm and guided her upward, but
her legs, on which she'd been sleeping for at least an hour,
wouldn't cooperate.

Abby gave an embarrassed laugh. "I'll just spend the
night down here."

Stephen took off his jacket and laid it over the arm of
the sofa. "And have the children wake you at six on a
Sunday morning? It looks like I'll have to do to you what
I do to Daphne." In one swift and smooth move, he
scooped her up into his arms. A barely audible cry of surprise came from deep in her throat. "Put your arms around
my neck," he ordered.

He carried her quickly across the living room and up the

stairs. She thought for a moment she must still be dreaming, but the woodsy scent of his aftershave was all too real, the heat of his muscular shoulder against hers too intense.

He stopped at her bedroom door and let her down gently. Her legs, though weak from lack of circulation and now weak from being in his arms, held her up—barely.

"Good night, Abby," he said in hushed tones. "Sweet dreams."

Chapter Five

Stunned, Abby sat on the edge of her bed. Her heart beat in a wild rhythm. Her arms throbbed where they had rested on the broad expanse of his shoulders. Her waist and the backs of her knees burned where his arms had encircled her body with strength and ease. To him, it had been no more than an act of courtesy, done partly in jest. To her, it was an unsettling reminder that despite her determination to keep him out, he was too much in her heart and mind.

For Stephen, it seemed uncharacteristically impulsive, against the grain of his normally reserved demeanor. The evening of dinner and dancing must have pleased him. There was a spark about him that wasn't there before.

Abby wriggled out of her leggings and pulled her sweater over her head. She slipped into a silk and lace floor-length gown of unknown vintage that she'd found in an English secondhand shop. Finely made, it had originally come from Harrod's. Because of a small tear near the hem, it had been a real bargain. She slid into bed and covered

herself with the patchwork quilt. But the chill deep inside her wouldn't go away.

Peter's birthday party was four days away and there was yet no end to the details to be worked out. The mothers of the neighborhood children had been contacted and told of the surprise party. To make sure that the secret would be kept, Abby and the mothers agreed that the young guests wouldn't be told of the celebration until a few moments beforehand.

She'd booked Chipper the Clown, Munch the Magician having had a previous engagement at a Cub Scout party. In the meantime, Peter had been led to believe that there would be simply a quiet family dinner at home. But there was still the meal to plan, the cake to order, and the decorations to be selected and hung. Mrs. Johnson, who came in once a week for the major housecleaning, would get the house in order. But Abby, with her regular duties attending to the children, felt herself slipping behind. She was still impeded somewhat by her wrist. Although the bandage was off and the doctor said it was healing nicely, she was to avoid lifting heavy objects.

In the meantime, Stephen was facing a project deadline and was scheduled to make a business trip to Oregon the night before the party. He wouldn't be back until the following afternoon. Mrs. Bybee was still spending most of her time with her daughter. Abby was determined not to ask either for help. That left only Kendall.

Kendall, Abby learned, ran a small philanthropic foundation that her parents had started. Since it wasn't terribly demanding, it allowed her enough free time for social activities. She could also leave the office whenever Stephen

needed her. Although Abby sensed that Kendall didn't consider her an equal, she called her, but there was no answer.
She left a recorded message.

It was Stephen, not Abby, to whom Kendall returned the
call. Abby had just returned from a walk with the children
when Stephen called her into his study.

He sat at a drafting table, the sleeves of his denim shirt
rolled up. His hair fell over his forehead and his lower lip
jutted out in concentration. Abby, who had been trying especially hard to maintain a detached demeanor since he'd
carried her to her room, felt her composure slip.

He glanced over her shoulder as if to be sure the children
weren't within earshot.

"Kendall would be delighted to help you with the
party," he said quietly.

"That's very nice of her," Abby said, trying not to be
distracted by his clear, gray gaze.

"What would you like for her to do?"

"Perhaps she could come the morning of the party and
help me hang the decorations and tend to some other details," she replied. "We can do it while the children are in
school."

"I'll call her tonight."

"That will be fine, sir." Her English formality was in-
tended to hide any trace of interest. She turned to leave the
room, but he called her back.

"Abby," he said, "I'm sorry if I was being too playful
last night, or rather this morning. I didn't mean to overstep
any bounds. I only meant to help you up the stairs. Under
the circumstances, that seemed to be the simplest way to
do it."

She looked into his eyes for the barest of moments, then
diverted her gaze to the sketch in front of him—an office

building with odd angles and other futuristic details. "It's quite all right. I took it for what it was—a show of consideration. I'm sorry to have incapacitated myself in that way, Mr. Kraft."

"Nonsense," he replied. A short pause followed. "What do you think of it?" he asked, placing a large, square hand on the drawing.

"Very nice. It looks like the twenty-first century has already arrived."

His eyes brightened. "That is exactly the statement I would like this building to make," he said. "It will be the headquarters of a technology company."

"It must be rewarding to have your name on a bronze plaque on the front of a building," she said.

He toyed with his drafting pencil for a moment, turning it over and over. "It used to be everything," he said. "But once Peter and Daphne were born, my perspective changed. Architecture is still important, but now they're the driving force inside me."

Abby's eyes locked on his in a moment of admiration and mutual understanding. She quickly turned away, fearful of revealing too much of herself to him. "I mustn't keep you," she said. "Good night, Mr. Kraft."

He put down his pencil. "You can call me Stephen."

She looked at him in surprise. "Yes, sir."

"And stop calling me 'sir.' "

"Yes, sir," she said.

Two days later, he was in Oregon, but being out of sight didn't put him out of mind. Not that she didn't try. She'd already known that swooping her up into his arms had been simply a spontaneous act with no meaning. His request that she call him by his first name likely meant only that he was no longer concerned that he might become the object of her affections.

She smiled at the bitter irony of it. She played her professional role better than she suspected. But her dealings with her employer—which ranged from benign to cheeky—were just that: an act. She spent hours silently lecturing herself and channeling her thoughts in any direction except toward him. But despite her best efforts, something inside her stirred when he entered the room. It was simply chemistry, she told herself. It was then that she realized that Kendall should be regarded as an ally. Not only did she curtail Stephen's availability, but there was a constant reminder that Abby's heart was beating foolishly.

By the eve of the party, Abby had taken care of many of the details except hanging the decorations and getting the food ready. Since Stephen wasn't there to help with the children, she was more tired than usual. While they were in school, she'd managed to buy Peter a book entitled *Tyrannosaurus Tex*, about a dinosaur cowboy. She was delighted that the topic that had given her so much pleasure as a child had captured his interest as well.

At ten-thirty on the morning of the party, there was no sign of Kendall. Glancing periodically at her watch, Abby busied herself with the streamers, twisting together colorful strips of crepe paper until her wrist began to ache. She called the foundation again, but there was no answer. Finally, she dialed the Vanderburg home.

"Oh, dear me," Mrs. Porter, Kendall's housekeeper, said. "She left around eight-thirty, saying something about the Society League, then picking up some clothing and going on to the beauty shop."

Abby's heart fell. "I hope she hasn't forgotten she was to help me decorate for the party."

There was a split second of silence on the other end of the line. "She didn't mention anything about it."

Abby's disappointment turned into annoyance. "I hope she hasn't forgotten Peter's birthday party."

"Oh, no," Mrs. Porter said. "In fact, she asked me this morning if I would go out and buy a gift, since I have grandchildren, you know . . ."

Abby's stomach tightened. "Thank you, Mrs. Porter," she said. "Please tell her I called."

"Of course, dear."

Abby hung up in frustration. Not only should Kendall be here, she thought, but she should have taken pleasure in selecting Peter's gift herself.

Abby went back to her decorating tasks, her anxiety building. She still had to pick up the cake, fetch the children from school, and organize the games the children would play. She worked as quickly as she could, finishing up the streamers and blowing up dozens of balloons with a rented pump. She glanced nervously at her watch. In an hour, it would be time to pick up Daphne. She'd planned on having the decorations hung by now.

A half hour later, the doorbell rang. Abby dropped the tape she was using to hang a game of "Pin the Tail on the Donkey," and rushed to answer it. Kendall stood on the threshold, her blond hair appearing to be freshly cut and styled. "Hello, Abby," she said brightly. "I'm sorry not to get here sooner. There are just so many things to do and so little time in which to do them."

"Please come in." Abby strained to keep her tone friendly. "I welcome your help."

She led her into the dining room where two dozen streamers lay everywhere. "We need to hang these from the ceiling, and from the streamers, we hang the balloons."

Kendall's eyes widened. "You went all out, didn't you?" she asked. "I didn't realize it would be so involved."

"It's Peter's big day," Abby responded simply.

Using ladders, they'd hung the streamers and half the balloons when Abby realized it was almost time to pick up Daphne. "Kendall, would you mind terribly if I asked you to fetch Daphne from preschool?"

Kendall brushed a speck from the sleeve of her white silk blouse. "I'm afraid I have an appointment, Abby. Perhaps I can come back before the party and help."

Abby worked to conceal her disappointment. "Thank you, Kendall. I would be grateful if you would."

Kendall returned at four o'clock, moments before Stephen's return from Oregon. Abby, weary from the nonstop preparations, asked her to watch the children while she took a shower and dressed for the party. When she entered the living room, wearing her black tent dress, a string of pearls, and black pumps with little heels, she found Stephen standing beside Kendall, his white shirt rumpled from travel. His briefcase and several blueprint tubes lay on the floor. The sight of him caused her blood to surge.

"Hello, Abby," he greeted her with a smile. "You look nice."

"Thank you," she said, taking note of how close Kendall was standing to him.

"Kendall said all is well."

"Yes," Abby said. "How was your trip? The children missed you." She looked slightly past Stephen to find them playing with the kitten.

"The design for the building I showed you the other night was approved, so I guess I can say it was a success."

"Now we have something else to celebrate besides Peter's birthday," Abby said.

Kendall hooked her arm through Stephen's. "Come in the dining room. I'll show you what Abby and I have been doing."

She opened the double doors to reveal a ceiling with a thick webbing of streamers and balloons. On the table were clown placements, silverware, glasses, and a bright arrangement of red and yellow tulips. Abby had managed all the rest after Kendall had left.

Stephen emitted a chuckle of delight. "This is terrific. You're both wonderful to do this."

Abby waited for a disclaimer from Kendall, but there was none. Her only response was to give Stephen's arm a squeeze.

"It was fun," Abby said with all the cheer she could gather.

The five of them sat down to Peter's favorite meal of spaghetti and meatballs. Just before dessert, just as Abby had planned, the doorbell rang.

"Peter, would you mind seeing who's at the door?" she asked benignly.

The boy dashed out of the room and a moment later, a chorus of children's voices could be heard shouting, "Surprise!"

Abby felt a swell of delight. Stephen and Kendall looked at each other and laughed. In an instant a beaming Peter was back in the dining room, leading a group of excited children.

"I've never had a surprise like this before!" Peter said, his eyes alight.

"Well, now you have," Stephen said, casting a knowing smile toward Abby.

Abby distributed a stack of plates from the dining room hutch and helped Stephen get the children settled. They included the Morgan twins, Brent and Kent, from next door; Suzie Myers, a six-year-old tomboy from across the street; and Bobby Adams and his little sister Annie from down the block.

Kendall went to the kitchen and returned with the cake, which Abby had ordered and had barely managed to pick up before the party. It was a European-style white confection decorated with cherries and a mound of shaved chocolate. In the center were seven candles. Kendall set it in front of Peter with aplomb.

"Happy seventh," she said.

"Make a wish and blow out the candles," Stephen added.

The little boy stood quietly over the cake for a moment, looked at Abby, and then at his father. Then with one deep, quick breath, the candles were out. The children applauded.

They delved into the cake, then the gifts were opened. Daphne watched intently as she stood next to her brother, her eyes barely above the tabletop. There was an assortment of toys, a computer game from Stephen, and a rooster alarm clock from Kendall.

"It goes cock-a-doodle-doo," she explained.

Stephen examined it and laughed.

"Thanks, Aunt Kendall," Peter said.

"You're more than welcome, dear," she said sweetly.

Abby's gift of the story of *Tyrannosaurus Tex* brought a smile. "Wow, I can't wait to read this."

"You're going to have to wait, because Chipper the Clown is here," Abby announced.

She stood in the background as the clown went through a routine of pantomime and juggling. Stephen and Kendall had also moved away, giving the children full view. It was then that Abby noticed that Stephen had slipped his arm around Kendall's waist.

During the remaining moments of the party, the image burned in her mind, despite her best efforts to erase it. As the children scattered for home, each with a handful of balloons taken from the ceiling, she stood with Peter at the door, making sure every child was properly thanked.

She turned back into the house with a mixture of fatigue and relief. The party had been a success. The children's laughter and the glow on Peter's face had told her that. What more could she ask for?

From the center hallway, Abby could see Kendall and Stephen in the living room. A glance into the dining room showed that Peter was still admiring the gifts. The room was a riot of crumpled gift-wrapping and ribbon and plates that needed washing. The sight of it brought another pang of fatigue. Yet it was a happy sort of weariness, because she knew all her work and planning had pleased him.

She began picking up the wrapping, enlisting the children's help.

"Can I have a birthday party, too?" Daphne asked.

She touched the little girl's tousled curls. "I'm sure it will be all right with your father, but you'll have to wait a while. Your birthday isn't until spring."

"Will you get me a pink cake?"

Abby felt a little twinge of sadness. It didn't seem the time to remind Daphne that she would be gone. "I'm sure it could be arranged," she said with a forced smile.

Abby heard the click of heels on the marble tile in the hallway and turned to find Kendall walking toward her. She was hoping for an offer of help, but instead, Kendall paused at the antique hall tree, took a piece of paper and a pen from her sleek leather shoulder bag, and scribbled a note. She folded it, then slipped it into the pocket of Stephen's old cardigan, which hung on its customary peg. She turned with a flourish and stepped into the dining room.

"It was a wonderful party, Abby," she said. "You've got quite a knack with children."

"Thank you," Abby replied. "I appreciate your help."

"Anytime," Kendall said sweetly. "Don't hesitate to ask."

Stephen appeared in the doorway. "Abby, I've just checked on Boom and given him his supper."

"That's thoughtful of you," she said. She turned toward the children. "Don't forget to give Boom a little extra attention this evening. He was probably bewildered by all the commotion from the party."

Daphne scampered toward the door, but Stephen intercepted her. "First, say good-bye to Aunt Kendall."

Kendall gave each of the children a hug, then Stephen followed her to the door.

About fifteen minutes later, Stephen came into the kitchen where Abby had just finished loading the dishwasher. But she still had hours to go before order could be made of the disorder left behind by eight children, three adults, a cat, and a clown.

"Sit down," Stephen said. She was startled by the firm tone of his order.

Too tired to argue, she complied. He sat across from her. Over his shoulder, she could see the children playing with the kitten in the television room. She sat in nervous expectation.

"You're wonderful to do all this for Peter," he said. "He'll remember this for a long time. What I'd like for you to do now is go up to your room and relax. I'll tend to the children.''

"But Mr. Kraft . . ." she protested.

"Stephen," he corrected, giving her a chiding look.

"Stephen," she said, the name seeming somehow forbidden on her lips, "I'll manage. I'm fine. I'm not the one who just flew in from a trip."

"No, but you're the one who is supposed to follow my instructions." His eyes glinted with determination.

"It's kind of you to take over," she said. "I'll make it up to you."

"Good night, Abby," he said.

"Good night, Stephen." She turned, but before she could exit the kitchen, Peter called Stephen's name and hers. He stood in the door holding his new copy of *Tyrannosaurus Tex.*

"I can read almost the whole first page by myself," he announced.

"Let me hear you, then," Stephen said, giving Abby a knowing glance. He pulled the boy into his lap. Before Peter could start, Daphne ran into the room, the cat close behind.

"Peter won't tell me what his birthday wish was," she complained.

"It's said that if you tell, it won't come true," Abby explained gently.

The little girl's chin crinkled. "I know what I'm going to wish on *my* birthday!" she exclaimed.

"Tell us," Stephen said, his tone filled with exaggerated interest.

"I want," she announced assuredly, "a mommy."

Chapter Six

Abby's heart thumped. She looked uneasily at Stephen. The color in his face deepened. His mouth opened, but he seemed unable to speak. Finally, he reached out and pulled Daphne onto his lap.

"You weren't hoping to get a mommy so soon, were you?" he asked, his voice low.

The little girl nodded.

Stephen glanced at Abby, his smile bittersweet. Suddenly, she felt like an intruder in a scene scripted only for a father and daughter. She turned to leave.

"Abby, don't good mommies take time to find?" he asked.

"Yes, they do," she replied.

"You see, Daphne, it has to be someone who thinks you and Peter are the most special children in the world. It has to be someone who likes me, too." he added wryly. He glanced at Abby, his eyes glinting with irony. "As your nanny can attest, the latter would be the biggest challenge."

"What does that mean, Daddy?" the little girl asked.

"What I'm really trying to say is that I can't make any promises and that you should be patient. We might not find anyone this year or next or maybe not for a long, long time. But I can tell you I'll do some serious thinking about it."

Daphne put her chubby arms around his neck and buried her face in his neck. Then she slid down from his lap and walked slowly back to the TV room. Abby detected a trace of disappointment in her step.

A pained look crossed his handsome face. "Diane has been dead less than two years," he said softly. "Now I realize that within the context of their lives, they've been without a mother for a long time."

Abby felt a strong urge to reach out and touch his shoulder, but she didn't dare.

"You're doing admirably well with the children," she said, regretting that words could do little to left the burden in his heart.

"Thank you, Abby," he said with a faint smile. "Now, don't let me keep you from rest any longer."

When Abby went downstairs the next morning, she found the dishes put away and the kitchen in order, except for the napkins in the silverware drawer and the spaghetti pot on top of the refrigerator. A large whisk also hung upside down from its hook. But the countertops sparkled and the pine table radiated a mellow glow. Stephen was too hard to be around when he was this nice, she thought as she hung the whisk right side up. She almost preferred his brusqueness.

She wore her black Doc Marten oxfords, at which she'd seen him cast a wary look in the past, a pair of faded jeans, an oversize vest that once went with a man's pinstripe suit, a floral-print tie, and a white shirt. Only this morning, she'd noticed a tear at the elbow. It was just as well. She didn't want Stephen to think that she was trying to impress anyone, especially him.

She set out the cereal bowls, poured the orange juice, plugged in the toaster, and put on the kettle for tea. In a half hour, she would wake the children. Only this time, they would likely be up before she got there because Stephen had promised to set the rooster alarm. Perhaps it was best after all that Kendall had left the gift-buying to her housekeeper, Abby thought ruefully. Peter had been delighted with it.

She stood by the French doors and studied the mist veiling the trees outside. The sky was the color of tin and the chill seemed to permeate the walls of the house. It was an English sort of chill, she thought wistfully. She touched her fingers to the panes of the door. Today, there was a hint of winter.

She heard footsteps behind her and turned. Stephen, dressed in gray corduroy pants, a light blue denim shirt, and a woolen maroon tie, stood in the kitchen doorway. His eyes flicked over her in casual interest.

"Good morning, Annie Hall."

She smiled wryly. "Abby will do."

He stepped up to her and touched her elbow. "You've a tear in your sleeve."

Her skin tingled from his touch. "Yes, I know," she said, avoiding his eyes. "One of the hazards of being Secondhand Rose. But it's a hand-tailored shirt of Egyptian cotton—quite nice, once."

As his eyes danced over it, Abby felt the color in her cheeks deepen. "Nice, once, but I'm afraid its day is past."

Abby fingered the tear self-consciously, but said nothing. There was a brief pause.

Stephen rubbed his upper arms. "It seems a bit chilly in here. Or perhaps with your being English you don't feel it. Or even more typically English, you do feel it, but you're not going to do anything about it. You're simply going to endure it."

Abby cast him a wary glance. "You're making light of my country again."

His mouth twitched with the barest hint of a smile. "I'm sorry. It's just that I try not to suffer unless I can help it."

Abby gave him a scolding with her eyes. "It was once said that the sun never sets on the British Empire. The empire wasn't built by sitting at home by the fire."

He rolled his eyes toward the ceiling. "I suppose I'd better put on a sweater, and while I'm on my way, I'll turn up the thermostat just a degree or two. I wouldn't want to drain our national oil reserves."

Abby responded with an irreverent quirk in the corner of her mouth. For her, the temperature in the room had already risen.

As he left the room, she nervously busied herself in the kitchen. Two years of nanny training had given her the ability to handle virtually every situation that could arise. But there was nothing in the textbooks about how to handle a man like Stephen Kraft.

A few moments later, he returned, wearing his baggy old cardigan and a look of satisfaction. Saying nothing, he helped her set the table.

"I hope you're all toasty warm now," she said, her voice tinged with irony.

"I'm beginning to thaw," he responded, thrusting his hands deep into the pockets of the sweater.

It was then that Abby remembered Kendall's slipping something into one of the pockets. An instant later, Stephen pulled out a scrap of paper. A puzzled look crossed his face. As he unfolded it, Abby detected a slight tremor in his hand.

He read what appeared to be a brief message, then he took a deep breath. He suddenly seemed lost in thought.

"Anything wrong?" Abby asked tentatively.

"Just a little note from Kendall." He opened it, studied it again, then refolded it.

Abby bit her bottom lip. She was seized by curiosity, but said nothing.

Suddenly a faint crowing rang through the air. "The alarm clock," Stephen said with a smile.

"I'll get the children," Abby said, heading toward the stairs.

About fifteen minutes later, she returned with Peter and Daphne, who were outfitted in the clothing she'd laid out the night before. Boom, who now slept in a basket in Daphne's room, rode in the crook of Daphne's arm.

Stephen kissed each of them. Daphne insisted he kiss Boom as well. He complied by kissing the kitten on the head. Before they sat down to breakfast, Abby couldn't help but notice that Stephen had removed the note from his pocket and looked at it again. As Peter talked of the field trip his class was to take, Stephen seemed uncharacteristically distracted.

While the children gathered their things for school, Abby sat next to him as he mulled over his coffee.

"Is everything okay?" she asked.

He sighed. "I momentarily encountered a ghost from the past. Diane had a funny habit—sweet, really—of putting little notes in the pockets of my jackets. Sometimes, it was simply, 'I love you.' Other times, it might be a little joke, a poem, or something nonsensical. For a moment, I thought it was from her. It took a few moments for it to register that this was from Kendall.''

Before she could respond, the children were back in the kitchen ready to be taken to school.

Stephen looked at his watch. "We'd all better hurry," he said, getting up.

Abby spent the morning doing the children's laundry, but she couldn't help but wonder about the note. Kendall's interest in Stephen was now crystal clear. But her interest in the children wasn't as well demonstrated. Then there was another haunting thought: How did Stephen feel about Kendall? Suddenly, the day seemed even grayer.

She forced her thoughts back to the children. Daphne was outgrowing her small assortment of overalls. The little girl had also outgrown her sole dress, which Abby guessed had been purchased by Mrs. Bybee. It was time to take Daphne shopping.

Abby picked her up at preschool, put on a pot of homemade stew for supper, picked up Peter, and by then it was almost time for Stephen to come home. Just before five-thirty, the car appeared in the driveway.

A few of her Norland classmates had complained that their employers didn't spend enough time with their children, that the children ranked second to the parents' careers and social interests. But with Stephen Kraft, his children came first. Rather than staying late at the office to meet a deadline, he worked at home, waiting until after the children had gone to bed to finish his work.

The children, who had been drawing at the kitchen table, threw down their crayons and rushed to the front door. What followed was a scene that always made Abby's heart jump. The instant the door opened, the children were in his arms. Abby wasn't sure what triggered the erratic beating of her heart—the sight of Stephen or the children's greeting.

"Hello, Abby," he said, striding toward her, carrying Daphne. "How was your day?"

"That's supposed to be *my* line," she said.

The corners of his mouth crinkled into a trace of a smile. "Everything was fine. How are things here at home?"

"Very well," she said. "The children's laundry is done and I managed to make a pot of stew. I hope you like it. It's my Aunt Margo's recipe."

"It certainly smells good," he said, putting Daphne down. "Let me change clothes and I'll help."

"It's not necessary," she protested. But it was too late. He'd already started up the stairs.

A few minutes later, he came into the kitchen wearing a faded denim shirt, chinos, and an old pair of loafers. Even in casual clothing, there was an air of formality about him. He stood in the doorway with his hands behind him as Abby stirred the stew.

"Abby," he said, "I have something for you."

She gave him a curious glance and put down her spoon. He produced a crisp, white shirt.

She looked at it in surprise, suddenly realizing that her mouth was open.

"Take it," he urged. "It's not Egyptian cotton or handmade, but it's guaranteed secondhand. I've worn it at least twenty times."

"But, why . . . ?" She took it with hesitation. The starched fabric felt cool against her fingers.

"You don't have to go around with tears in your elbows, Egyptian cotton tears though they may be."

Abby gave him a slightly embarrassed smile. "Thank you very much." She couldn't help but think of the intimacy of wearing something of his, of feeling the texture of the pinpoint oxford cloth against her body. She turned away in fear that he might be able to read her thoughts.

"By the way," he said wryly, "it's freshly laundered."

She turned back toward him. "That has been duly noted."

That evening, after the children had been put to bed, Stephen met her at the foot of the stairs with a cup of hot chocolate. She took it with surprise.

"Come in the living room," he said. "I have a proposal for you."

Her heart racing, she followed him into the living room. She sat on the sofa across from him as she had the night they'd met. Only now, he wasn't so much given to brooding and his stiff facade was beginning to soften.

She sipped the chocolate. It was creamy and rich. "I'm impressed."

"Don't be," he said. "It came out of an envelope."

"In that case, it's the thought that counts."

"Try this thought," he said leaning forward. "How would you like several days off?"

Her heart fluttered in surprise.

"You've been with us for nearly a month and you've hardly taken a moment for yourself. I have some friends, the Carringtons, who are retired and live in the mountains. They were friends of my mother's. I thought I'd take the children there this weekend. Peter likes to fish in the stream and Daphne likes playing with their Yorkshire terriers. We haven't been there in a while. Kendall will be going, too. This will give her an opportunity to spend more time with the children."

Abby's surprise gave way to a heavy feeling. "Certainly," she said, pushing cheer into her voice. "I'll see to it that the children's things are ready."

"Don't make too much of a fuss," he said. "Make some plans for yourself. Take the car, do some shopping, do anything you like. But please make an effort to relax and enjoy yourself."

The initial excitement that Abby felt began to wane. Yes, she would enjoy some time to herself, but the prospect of two days and nights stretching before her suddenly made her feel alone. And in Seattle, she knew hardly a soul.

They left on Friday afternoon. Abby made sure that the children had all the proper clothing, that each had taken a favorite toy, and that they were properly buckled into the backseat of the minivan. She promised Daphne that she would take good care of Boom, and kissed them both good-bye.

She felt a little tug at her heart as Stephen backed out of the driveway with a wave. She stood on the sidewalk until the car disappeared from view.

She treated herself to a pizza delivered to the door and settled down with a new mystery book, but she felt oddly unsettled. It was good that Kendall would be able to spend more time with the children, she told herself. Yet it didn't take away her feelings of uneasiness. The memory of Kendall handling the children's artwork with casual abandon flashed through her mind. Then there was Peter's cherished alarm clock that he thought his aunt had chosen with care.

Her appetite suddenly vanishing, she pushed the pizza away. The note that Kendall had placed in Stephen's pocket had certainly been an endearing one. She was afraid for Stephen, that his heart might be led astray by a woman who looked so much like Diane. She feared Daphne's wish for a mother might influence him to reach out to someone before it was time. And she was afraid for herself, afraid of the meaning of the wild beating of her heart every time he walked through the door.

Early Saturday morning, she awoke with a start until she remembered that Daphne and Peter were gone. She sank back against the pillows.

Daphne, who was usually good-natured, had pouted a bit when she'd learned Abby wouldn't be going to the mountains with them. Stephen had convinced her that everyone needed a little vacation, including nannies.

Peter had "loaned" her his copy of *Tyrannosaurus Tex* for the weekend—in case she "needed something good to read."

Abby smiled at the thought of them. They were such lovely children. She was already hopelessly attached.

Too tense to rest, she scrambled out of bed. She reached down and stroked Boom, whose basket had been moved into her room. He emitted a soft purr. After splashing water on her face, she pushed back the louvered folding doors of her closet. Hanging in the center was the white shirt Stephen had given her. She touched its soft folds and her heart skittered. She hadn't yet worn it. It seemed somehow forbiddingly intimate. But she knew that he expected her to wear it as if it were nothing more than a hand-me-down from an older brother.

She slipped her old silk gown over her shoulders and let it fall in a puddle around her ankles. She took the shirt from the hanger and put it on. The stiff, cool fabric made her bare skin tingle.

She slowly buttoned it, the cuffs covering all but her fingertips. She rolled up the sleeves and pressed one against her face. It smelled faintly of evergreen. It smelled like Stephen.

A feeling of foolishness and embarrassment suddenly came over her. She quickly undid the shirt and hung it back in the closet, pushing it out of view.

Her clothing was an eclectic assortment that included almost nothing that was new. There was a Navy pea coat; one of her father's Air Force dress shirts, complete with epaulets; a pair of black velvet Capri pants; a red chemise that the clerk in a quaint shop had said was from the Twenties; a peach wool miniskirt and dyed-to-match sweater from the late 1960s; a short red bellman's jacket with gold braid; a chef's smock; a tuxedo shirt with black tie; and a kimono. She threw on the chef's smock and a pair of jeans. She gave her dark hair a quick brush and secured it with a black velvet headband.

Downstairs, the house was eerily quiet. Her footsteps seemed to echo across the kitchen floor. She took Boom outside, then settled down to a breakfast of porridge, toast, and tea. The children had recently started calling their oatmeal ''porridge,'' a development that Stephen had seemed to find amusing.

''What's next?'' he'd asked. ''Curds and whey?''

Everything she did made her think of them. She tried to concentrate on something else, but her thoughts always came back to the children. She missed Daphne's inquiring blue eyes and her tousled curls. She missed Peter's quiet seriousness. For seven, he seemed so very grown up until she read to him. Then the little boy, who put on such a strong and protective facade for his little sister, rested his head against her shoulder as if seeking for himself a protective and maternal touch.

Her bonding to them had begun almost from the start.

The pull had been almost as strong as her antipathy toward their father. She stared into her empty teacup and took a deep breath. What was wrong with her? This shouldn't be happening.

She spent the rest of the day away from the house. She went to several vintage clothing shops with the intention of getting her mind off the Krafts, but instead she came away with a dress for Daphne. It was a red plaid with a white collar, puffed sleeves, and a sash that tied into a bow in the back. It reminded her, as Daphne did, of Sally in the "Dick and Jane" reader from her father's boyhood.

That afternoon, at a used-book store, she picked up some dinosaur books for Peter, then stepped inside a coffee bar for cappuccino. She was hoping the hum of conversation about her would detract her from her thoughts, but instead she felt more alone.

That evening, after a quick supper of scrambled eggs and toast, she settled on the sofa with Boom and answered her latest letter from Aunt Margo. She promised that before she went back to England, she would visit Tumbleweed Ranch. On Sunday, she took a long walk through the fallen leaves. The day, like Saturday, had been a surprisingly long one.

At mid-afternoon, the minivan appeared in the driveway and Abby's heart responded with a kick. Peter was out of the car before Stephen could get Daphne out of her child seat. Peter ran to Abby, presenting her with a soggy brown-paper bag. "I brought you something!" he exclaimed.

She peered inside and responded with an exaggerated expression of surprise. She found two small pieces of quartz.

"Jewels!" he said excitedly.

"How lovely!" she said. "How very thoughtful of you. I will keep them safe in my jewelry box."

Stephen turned to her with a crooked grin. Before she could say anything, Daphne bounded toward her. Abby lifted her into her arms. "Bears live in the woods and they eat people's lunches," the little girl announced.

"Indeed they do," Abby said, kissing her cheek. "I hope you had a jolly good time. I missed you." She put the child down and watched her run into the house after her brother.

Stephen walked toward her. His hair was windblown, his cheeks tinged with the outdoors. "I don't suppose you missed me," he said, a hint of a smile on his lips.

"I managed without you," she said wryly.

"I'm certain you did." He casually put his arm around her shoulder and led her into the house. His touch caused her heart to leap.

"Did you have a lovely time?" she asked. She had to wait until he removed his arm before she could get her breath.

"Perfectly lovely, as you would say."

They went into the kitchen where the children were playing with the cat. Stephen sat down as Abby put on a pot of tea.

"We all went on a hike," he said, "although I had to carry Daphne partway. Peter was intrigued. He kept looking for arrowheads and anything that might have been a dinosaur bone. You've got him quite worked up about dinosaurs. You might be pleased to know that the Carringtons were impressed that Peter knew so much about the different types of them."

Abby responded with a smile.

"We cooked most of our meals outside on the deck," he continued. "Kendall loved it and she enjoyed being with the children. I want them to become closer. After all, we're sort of a family."

She nodded and smiled bravely, but inside she felt the cold, sharp blade of fear.

"Kendall told them stories about their mother when she was a little girl," he continued. "They especially enjoyed that."

"Yes, they would," Abby said with a brightness she didn't feel. She went to the stove and poured Stephen a cup of tea. For the children's sake, she hoped that Kendall truly enjoyed being with them, that she wasn't thinking only of Stephen.

"Abby, I've been thinking," Stephen said, toying with the rim of his cup. The evening light from the French doors brought out the square lines of his jaw. "I'd like to have a real Thanksgiving this year, bring out the good china and the silver and have all the traditional things. It would just be you, the children, and Kendall and me."

For a moment, Abby couldn't speak. She'd known that Thanksgiving had been a painful holiday for him, since it had been Diane's favorite. There had been a turning point in his life, and the turning point, she'd suspected, was Kendall.

"That would be very nice," she finally managed to say.

There was a brief pause. "Last year was sort of a bungled affair," he said. "Mrs. Bybee was with her family. Kendall spent the holiday with friends. Mrs. Bybee invited us to have Thanksgiving with her, but I felt we would be intruding. I also didn't think her daughter needed the noise and excitement of having extra children around. She wanted to cook the meal for us in advance, but I had it catered. I didn't want her to go to the trouble.

"As it turned out, it was a strange and lonely day. The dining room table seemed huge and empty with just the three of us. It didn't matter to Daphne, but Peter remembered celebrating Thanksgiving with his mother and grandparents at the table. I put up a brave front for the sake of the children, but it was difficult.''

Abby's heart ached. She struggled to maintain a neutral countenance. She didn't want Stephen to be embarrassed by her sympathy. ''I would be very happy to help you plan a Thanksgiving this year,'' she said.

''Wonderful,'' he said, his eyes brightening. Then he paused for a moment. ''You do know all about Thanksgiving, don't you?''

''Of course,'' she said. ''My life hasn't all been roast beef and Yorkshire pudding. Every year, my father bought a turkey at the post exchange. Every year, my mother managed to overcook it.''

His eyes danced with humor. ''Does overcooking turkeys run in the family?''

Abby cast him a wary look. ''I've never roasted one before, to be quite truthful.''

''It doesn't matter,'' he said, toying with the handle on his cup. The cup looked especially small and delicate next to his strong hand. ''Kendall and I will do as much as possible. We'd like to recreate a Vanderberg Thanksgiving menu. You won't need to worry about much of anything but the children.''

''But I wouldn't mind helping at all,'' she protested.

''This time,'' he said with a soft smile that caused her insides to melt, ''you're the guest.''

''That's quite kind of you,'' she said. But in her heart she knew that the holiday belonged to Stephen, Kendall, and the children, and that she was the outsider.

Chapter Seven

Thanksgiving morning was chilly and cloudy with an occasional ray of muted sunshine. For the holiday, Abby dressed Peter in a white shirt, black pants, and bow tie, and a red vest that she'd bought just days before. Daphne was outfitted in her vintage red plaid dress and white tights. Then Abby added the finishing touch—a red bow for her hair.

The little girl's eyes widened in delight as she stood before a full-length mirror.

"You look perfectly charming," Abby said, her heart spilling over with affection. She gave the child a quick hug. "Let's go show your father and your brother."

Daphne ran down the stairs in a blur, the sash ends of the bow at the back of her dress flying after her. Abby followed her into the living room where Stephen was reading the newspaper.

"Daddy, I look perfectly charming," she announced breathlessly.

Stephen put down the paper. His eyes flickered with

87

delight. "Charming can't begin to describe the way you look."

The little girl grinned as her father pulled her into his lap. He kissed her temple. "Abby, the children look wonderful today," he said. He cast his gaze at Peter, who sat on the sofa with a coloring book, then toward Abby.

Her cheeks tingled slightly. "Thank you. I couldn't agree more."

It was not quite nine o'clock, yet the smell of baking turkey was already beginning to fill the house. Abby peeped inside the oven to find it commencing nicely.

"Remember, you're the guest, not the cook."

She turned to find Stephen leaning against the kitchen doorway with his hands in his pockets. His white shirt was rolled up at the sleeves. The knot of his dark green foulard tie was loosened, his collar unbuttoned.

"Are you sure you don't need any help?" she asked. She thought of his earlier attempt at pancakes.

He looked at her wryly. "Kendall will be here at any moment," he said. "What I can't handle, she can. She's a bit of a gourmet. She took a cooking course in Paris last summer. In fact, this turkey is being baked according to her instructions."

Before she could respond, the doorbell rang. The children's footsteps echoed across the tiled entryway. Stephen, ever polite, excused himself and went to answer it. Abby stepped into the living room to find Kendall laden with large shopping bags. Stephen took them from her and kissed her cheek.

Kendall, who looked especially pretty in a red knit chemise that grazed the tops of her knees, knelt and kissed Peter, then Daphne. Her eyes lingered on the little girl for a moment, then met Abby's.

"Hello, Abby." Her tone, as usual, was cool and cultivated.

"Happy Thanksgiving, Kendall," Abby said. "Can I help you carry anything from the car?"

"Yes, thank you. As a matter of fact, you can."

"That won't be necessary," Stephen interjected as he returned from the kitchen. "I'll get the rest."

"That's sweet of you," Kendall said brightly. She took the children by the hand. "Come see what Aunt Kendall brought."

Abby, feeling slightly awkward, followed them into the kitchen. On the table was a copper pan of dressing rich with celery and eggs and smelling of sage. There was an earthenware pan of sliced sweet potatoes arranged like overlapping coins and sprinkled with candied ginger. There was a bag of fresh green beans, yet uncooked. The children peered at it excitedly.

"It looks delicious, Kendall," Abby said. "Such trouble you've gone to."

"For Stephen and the children, it was no trouble at all," she said.

Stephen entered the kitchen carrying a large pan covered with a brocade cloth. Just as he set it down, Peter lifted a corner of the cloth. Underneath were freshly baked rolls. Another container held homemade cranberry sauce.

"It was Mother's special recipe," Kendall said of the sauce.

"I'll go get the pies," Stephen said. Squealing, the children ran after him.

Abby watched, a poignant feeling spreading over her.

"Abby," Kendall said as soon as they were out of earshot, "about Daphne's dress."

Her stomach tightened. "Yes?"

"Where did you get it?"

"In a shop called Past Perfect."

Kendall frowned. "That's what I was afraid of. I don't like the idea of her wearing secondhand clothing."

Abby's cheeks grew warm. "Perhaps if I could explain . . . it's not simply secondhand. It's vintage. It's in very good condition."

Kendall looked at her with narrowed eyes. "Call it what you like. It's a cute dress and it looks very good on her, but it's used. Secondhand clothing is fine for someone without a lot of money or someone with, well . . . eclectic tastes such as yours, but Stephen can certainly afford new dresses for Daphne."

Abby's cheeks went from warm to searing hot. "If Stephen doesn't approve of my choice of clothing for Daphne, I would hope that he would let me know," she said, struggling to maintain an even tone. "I wouldn't want to do anything to displease him."

"I know you wouldn't," Kendall said with a stiff smile.

They were interrupted by the children bounding into the kitchen. Peter held a box and Stephen followed, carrying another. "They smell exquisite," Stephen said. He placed his on the table and took Peter's from him. He opened both boxes to reveal a pumpkin pie and a pecan tart. Abby intercepted Daphne's finger just before she could plunge it into the pumpkin custard. "After dinner, sweetheart," she said gently.

Stephen chuckled softly. "Abby, why don't you take the children for a little walk while Kendall and I get dinner ready?"

"That's a good idea," Abby said.

She took the children down the winding, tree-lined street on which they lived. Both of them ran ahead, kicking through the fallen leaves and stopping to throw handfuls of them into the air. The sun was peeping regularly through the clouds, slightly lifting Abby's spirits. The fire in her cheeks was all but gone, but she still felt the sting of Kendall's comment. She hoped Stephen didn't feel the same, but was too kind to tell her.

She suddenly yearned for her Aunt Margo. Today, she would be preparing a dinner for the ranch hands who didn't have families. She did it Texas style, smoking turkeys outdoors and throwing jalapeño peppers into everything. But most of all, Abby missed her father.

Ahead of her, the children bounded with energy, but Abby took care not to tire them. "Just another block or two," she admonished, "and we should start back."

At the end of the second block, a construction site with bulldozers and heavy equipment came into view.

"Wow!" Peter explained. "Let's go look."

"All right," she relented, seeing that it was just another block away.

It was the construction site for an elementary school. The land had been cleared a few days before. It was cordoned off for excavation.

"Do you suppose there could be dinosaur bones buried under there?" Peter asked. His eyes sparkled with curiosity.

"It's not likely, but the possibility is there," Abby replied.

"If only I could find a fossil or something," he said wistfully.

"I'm afraid the best place to look is in a museum," she said.

When they arrived at home, the dining room table was covered with a Battenburg lace cloth and set with china, silver, and gleaming crystal goblets. A centerpiece of yel-

low roses and baby's breath, which Abby had bought the
day before, was flanked by silver candlesticks. Abby followed the children as they hurried into the kitchen. She
took a deep breath, determined to keep up a cheerful facade.

Stephen swooped Daphne up in his arms. "Where did
you go, apple cheeks?" His eyes met Abby's. She blinked
to keep from losing herself in the startling clarity of them.

"We saw where they're going to build a new school,"
Peter interjected. "They're going to dig a big hole to put
it in. I want to see what they find in that dirt."

"They find rocks, mostly," Stephen said, "although I
remember during one excavation the workers found a steel
box containing some money."

Peter's eyes widened. "How much?"

"Just a few hundred dollars," Stephen said, "but con-
sidering the time it was probably buried, it was a lot."

"What did they do with it?"

Stephen grinned at his son in that crooked way that made
Abby's heart melt. "They did the proper thing. They turned
it over to the police."

"Oh," the little boy said, looking disappointed. "And
then what happened?"

"They couldn't determine the owner, so the new owners
of the land gave it to charity."

"Who's hungry?" Kendall interrupted as she stood at
the stove. Her cheeks were flushed from the heat of the
oven.

The children responded in a chorus.

"It won't be much longer," she said.

Abby took the children to wash their hands, and upon
her return to the kitchen, she found Kendall with one hand
on Stephen's shoulder. With the other, she fed him a spoon-

ful of dressing. Their faces were just inches apart. Abby's heart knocked uneasily against her ribs. Unnoticed, she quickly stepped back into the living room.

"I'm hungry," Daphne complained.

At that moment, Stephen stepped into the living room with a tray of appetizers. There were snow peas filled with cream cheese, salmon mousse on crackers, tiny quiches, and black and green olives. "There, little one," he said.

As the children munched contentedly, Kendall emerged from the kitchen with glasses of white wine.

Stephen held his glass up in a toast. "To happy holidays and happy memories," he said. He smiled softly at Kendall, then at Abby. Her blood stirred. Their glasses met, sounding a note of ringing crystal.

"Abby, are you looking forward to going back to England?" Kendall asked sweetly.

The question brought such a rush of conflicting emotions that, for an instant, she was speechless. "I will miss the children, but, of course, I miss England as well."

"Abby, do you have to go?" Daphne asked with a pout.

Abby reached over on the sofa and straightened the red bow in the little girl's hair. "Yes, sweetheart," she said. "Mrs. Bybee will be back and will take very good care of you."

While they finished their wine, they made small talk, but despite the cheer she tried to project, Abby's heart was heavy.

They sat down to a table laden with all the things that Kendall had made. The candles were lit and the room smelled of wax and freshly baked pies.

"This is wonderful, Kendall," Stephen said, sitting at the head of the table. Abby saw a rare sparkle in his eyes. She sat at his right and Abby at his left. Peter sat next to

Abby and his sister next to Kendall. "Let's give thanks, Peter," he said, reaching for Kendall's hand and Abby's. Abby's heart gave a little leap as his warm, strong fingers closed around hers. She in turn took Peter's hand. The little boy recited a short, child's prayer.

Abby was touched by the scene, thinking how differently things were now for the Kraft family. She wondered which chair had been Diane's and where the grandparents would have sat. But despite the tragedy, she was confident that the children would grow up to be strong and self-reliant. Stephen's qualities as a father impressed her deeply.

"This is the moment we've been waiting for," Stephen said, rising from his chair. He picked up a large knife and meat fork and began to carve the turkey.

Seeing their anxiousness, Abby began tending to the children's plates. She filled their goblets half full with milk and placed napkins across their laps. As she carefully explained which fork to use first, she could feel Kendall's eyes on her. But when she sat back down, it was Stephen whom Kendall was studying. There was a light in her eyes, one that Abby recognized. It was the look of a woman who cared for a man.

Abby reminded herself that her only concern should be the children, but it didn't take away the uneasy feeling in her heart.

Stephen placed small slices of turkey on the children's plates. "I tried my best," he said. "I hope the children don't remember this as the Thanksgiving of the rubber turkey."

"It looks perfect," Kendall said.

"I forgot to sharpen the knife," he said. "Excuse me while I step into the kitchen. Please start serving yourselves."

An awkward silence followed as Stephen left the room. "Everything is so lovely," Abby said finally.

"Thank you," Kendall said with a smile.

Self-consciously, Abby buttered rolls for the children. As she sat down again, she saw a flash of motion out of the corner of her eye. Kendall gasped and shot up from her chair. Abby turned to find Daphne's milk overturned and the front of Kendall's knit dress darkened with liquid. At the edge of the table was Daphne's overturned goblet. A spreading circle of milk soaked the tablecloth.

Abby ran to her side as Kendall quickly set the glass upright. "It's all right," Abby said, thrusting her crisply starched napkin at her. "Accidents happen."

Kendall's jaw stiffened as she blotted the stain. "Your glass goes on the right, Daphne," she said, her tone cross. She cast the little girl a reprimanding look with her perfectly made-up eyes. Daphne responded with a quiver of her bottom lip.

"It was just natural that she would try to put it on the left side of her plate," Abby explained, daubing at the tablecloth. "She's left-handed." She placed a hand on the child's shoulder. "We're very sorry it happened, aren't we, Daphne?"

"I didn't mean to spill it," the little girl said. There were tears in her voice. "I'm sorry."

At that moment, Stephen entered the room carrying the knife in one hand and the sharpener in the other. His eyes widened.

"A little spilled milk," Abby quickly explained, handing Kendall a fresh napkin. "Hardly anything to cry over."

A light little laugh came from Kendall. "It's almost funny."

Stephen's expression softened. "Thank you for being so

nice about it. With children, every moment is an adventure.''

"It will wash out fine," Abby said. "Would you like to change into something else? We're close to the same size."

"No, thank you," Kendall said with a graciousness that wasn't apparent moments ago. "It will be dry in no time."

"If . . . if you like, there are a few things of Diane's upstairs in the trunk at the foot of my bed," Stephen said. "I don't want you to be uncomfortable during dinner."

Kendall was silent for a moment, then she rose. "Perhaps you're right. I'll be right back. Please continue with dinner." On her way out of the room, she paused to give Daphne a kiss on the top of the head.

Abby sat down, her nerves taut. Her plate was still empty.

Stephen took her plate and placed several slices of turkey on it. "Fill your plate. It's time to think of yourself for a change."

Abby was suddenly conscious of soft music playing in the background. "The music is nice," she said.

"It soothes the savage breast," he said, his eyes sparkling with irony.

"A bout with savage-breast syndrome, have you?" She was deliberately contentious to hide her fragile emotions.

His mouth crooked in a half smile. "It comes and goes." He spread a piece of turkey with a fork and inspected it playfully. She was happy to see him in good spirits and that the holiday, after all, hadn't made him sad.

"By the way," he continued, "while I was up, I got the camera. When Kendall comes back, we'll take some pictures."

Before Abby could respond, Kendall appeared in the doorway wearing an ordinary black knit turtleneck dress with straight lines. It was a casual garment, but Kendall, with her sleek blond hair and reed-thin figure, gave it a look of sophistication.

Stephen paled at the sight of her. It was almost as if he'd seen a ghost. Abby's heart kicked at his reaction.

"A perfect fit," Kendall said, running a flawlessly manicured hand from her shoulder to her wrist.

Stephen's Adam's apple bobbed with a hard swallow. A moment seemed to pass before he could find his voice. "Very nice," he said finally.

"Thank you," she said softly.

Abby's food turned to paper in her mouth.

For the rest of the dinner, Stephen couldn't seem to keep his eyes off Kendall. After they took turns taking pictures, Abby tried to busy herself with the children. After they'd finished their desserts, she took them outside to play with the cat. When they came back into the house, Stephen and Kendall were still sitting at the dining room table.

"Not to interrupt, Stephen, but I'll be happy to do the washing up," Abby offered. "Perhaps you'd be more comfortable in the living room."

He turned toward her, his eyes beautifully clear. "That's nice of you, Abby, but please don't worry about a thing. Kendall and I will take care of it."

"I really don't mind at all," she said. "The children are watching cartoons." The truth was that she had to stay busy to distract herself from Stephen and Kendall. She was confused and troubled and knew that idleness would make things worse. Without waiting for a response, she began clearing the table.

"Really, Abby, you shouldn't have," Stephen said after Kendall left about an hour later.

She popped a dish towel back on its rack and managed

a smile. "I really didn't mind. I have trouble sitting still, you know."

He gave her one of his crooked grins that made her heart do a somersault. "Let's sit down a minute," he said, motioning toward the kitchen table. "I have a suggestion to make."

"I'll pour some tea," she said.

"*I'll* pour the tea," he commanded. "You sit."

Casting a look of annoyed compliance toward him, Abby did as she was told. She watched his fluid movements as he filled two cups and set them on the table. "I would never have thought that anyone could have made a tea drinker out of me," he said.

"Life is full of surprises."

His eyes sparkled over the rim of his cup.

"Abby, do you do anything for fun besides shopping for those interesting clothes of yours?"

Her cheeks tingled. "I like to read, if that's what you mean."

He smiled softly. "Abby, what I'm trying to say is that you're all work and no play."

"But my work *is* my play," she countered. "I enjoy being with the children."

He leaned forward, resting his elbows on the table. "Abby, please allow me to be more specific. Why isn't there a man in your life?"

She felt a twinge of surprise. "Should there be?"

He studied her for a moment, his eyes glinting with humor. "You're a pretty young woman, Abby. All that beauty and sass shouldn't go to waste."

She could feel the color in her cheeks deepen. "You're not talking to an old maid, you know."

The smile on his lips was almost imperceptible. "You still haven't answered my question."

She gave a sigh of impatience. "I hardly have time, in case you haven't noticed."

"Well, then," he said, his head cocked playfully, "I have a proposal for you."

Abby looked at him curiously, but said nothing.

"I'd like to show my appreciation to you for helping today—when you didn't have to—and for doing all the little extra things you do, such as giving Peter a birthday party. I'd like to treat you to something special."

"It's quite unnecessary," she protested.

"Please listen," he said, touching her sleeve. The heat of his fingers penetrated the cloth of her dress, warming her blood. "The Architecture Society's autumn ball is Saturday. I'd like for you to go with Kendall and me."

Abby stiffened. "But I couldn't possibly. Three's a crowd."

"What about four?"

She hesitated for a moment. "What do you mean?"

"There's someone I'd like you to meet," he said, gazing at her serenely. "There's a young architect working temporarily at my firm. Although I'm no judge of men's looks, the secretaries find him quite appealing. I'd like for both of you to come to the ball with us."

Abby nipped at the inside at her cheek.

"I know this may seem a little awkward for you at first, but I really think you'll have a good time," he said. "Greg is new in town and doesn't know anyone. You're new and you don't know anyone. He'd appreciate some company for the evening. He told me so."

Abby toyed nervously with her saucer. "It's very nice

of you to think of me, but I'm afraid I have nothing that would be appropriate to wear."

"Don't worry," he said. "Kendall has closets full of things. She'd be happy to loan you something. And don't worry about the children either. Mrs. Bybee will sit for a few hours."

Indecision gnawed at her. Spending an evening with Kendall and Stephen would be difficult, but she wanted to please him. Perhaps meeting someone was just what she needed. "Yes," she answered finally, "I would be pleased to go."

His face brightened. "You'll enjoy it, I promise. There will be a live orchestra and lots of good food."

"Stephen," she said hesitantly, "speaking of clothing. You don't mind Daphne wearing a secondhand dress, do you?"

"Not at all," he answered without hesitation. "She looks like an angel in it. Why did you ask?"

"I just wanted to be sure you approved," she said evasively.

"I do," he said, "very much. It was very thoughtful of you to buy it for her."

He looked at her with his clear, penetrating gaze and her heart yearned for that which she knew she could never have.

Chapter Eight

Abby pulled into the driveway after taking the children to a nearby shopping mall to see the Christmas decorations. Daphne had sat on the lap of an offbeat Santa in cowboy boots and given him a wish list—a dollhouse and a new mommy. At the latter, Abby's heart gave a little twist. It still amazed her that in America, the Christmas season began a month early, on the day after Thanksgiving.

But there was too much on her mind to think about Christmas. There was the Architecture Society ball.

She unloaded the children along with an inexpensive gift they'd bought for their father. It was a ten-dollar tie from a sale rack. Peter had been particularly impressed because the tie was illustrated with Disney cartoon characters. They had no money, but Abby made them a loan with the promise that they would work it off by doing odd jobs and running errands for her.

They'd barely gotten inside the front door when the telephone rang.

"Kraft residence. Abby speaking," she answered crisply.

"It's Kendall, Abby. I'd like to come by in a few minutes if you're free. I'll bring a ball gown." Her tone was polite, but guarded.

"Yes," Abby replied, twisting the phone cord nervously. "That would be quite nice."

Abby had settled the children at the kitchen table with graham crackers and mugs of hot chocolate when the doorbell rang. Before she could reach the front door, Kendall had already opened it with her own key. In one arm she carried a large, flat box bearing the name of a fashionable department store. She looked sleek and sophisticated in a long black coat.

"Hello, Kendall," Abby greeted. She tried her best to be cordial. "Please come in the kitchen. We're having an afternoon snack."

"Thank you," Kendall said, following Abby through the living room, "but I can only stay a moment."

Kendall breezed into the kitchen and set the box on the table. "It's a size seven. We can have it altered if it's not a perfect fit."

"Aunt Kendall!" the children chimed, vying for her attention.

"Hello, children," she said, rumpling their hair. She turned back to Abby. "Let me know if the gown fits okay."

"Of course," Abby said. "It's really very nice of you to bring it over."

"It was no problem at all."

"Why don't you stay for tea?"

Kendall glanced at a gleaming gold watch. "I'm really sorry, but I can't. I have some business to take care of. I'll see you on Saturday."

Abby felt a pang of disappointment on the children's behalf.

With scarcely a good-bye, Kendall was gone.

"Where is Aunt Kendall going?" Daphne asked at the snap of the front door. There were cracker crumbs on her cheeks.

"I don't know, pumpkin," Abby said. "I'm sure she had something very important to do."

"She's always busy," Peter added. "One time she was on TV. I saw her."

"What was she doing?" Abby asked.

"Oh, just talking," he said, swinging his legs.

Abby smiled at the bareness of his response.

"Open it, Abby," Daphne said, pointing at the box. "Is it a present?"

"No, your Aunt Kendall is loaning me a dress to go to the autumn ball. It's on the night Mrs. Bybee is coming to sit with you, remember?"

The little girl nodded. "Let me see," she said, leaning forward eagerly.

Abby carefully opened the box and parted the tissue paper. Inside was a gown of shimmering black taffeta. Her heartbeat quickened. She took it out and held it at arm's length. A large black bow graced one shoulder, and from there the bodice was cut, toga-style, along a diagonal line to create a gown that was half strapless. From the fitted waist flowed a gathered, bell-shaped skirt. Abby gasped. It was one of the most elegant gowns she'd ever seen. It must have cost hundreds of dollars, more than she could ever afford.

"It's beautiful," she said, holding it against her body. "What do you think, children?"

Peter shrugged disinterestedly. "It's a Cinderella dress," Daphne said, her eyes shining.

Abby could barely take her eyes off it. Her ambivalence

about going to the ball diminished. She would still feel a little awkward sharing an evening with Stephen and Kendall and a man whom she'd never met, but to wear such a gown would help put her at ease. Hesitantly, she folded it and put it back in the box, then set the box in the hallway so she could later take it upstairs.

As she turned to go back to the kitchen, the front door opened and Stephen entered. Abby noted that he had circles under his eyes. He dropped his briefcase by the door.

"You're home early," she said, surprised.

Suddenly, she heard the patter of children's footsteps across the kitchen floor and the slam of a door.

"What was that all about?" he asked.

For a moment, she was also confused until she remembered they hadn't yet hidden their father's Christmas gift. It had been lying on the kitchen table. Abby shrugged mysteriously.

Before he could respond, the children ran toward him, greeting him with kisses and hugs. The shadows under his eyes seemed to soften.

"What was all that commotion?" he asked.

Peter smiled cryptically. "Nothing."

Stephen looked warily at his son. "Remember what I said about running in the house?"

Peter nodded.

"All right, then." Abby noted a weariness in his normally steady baritone.

"Is everything all right?" she asked after the children had left in pursuit of Boom.

"We've been working all day to please a very cantankerous old dowager who refuses to be pleased. She's helping finance the wing of a hospital and insists on having everything done in pink along with special little chapels on each floor. The problem is that her ideas interrupt the flow of the floor plans. The hospital people don't like her taste either, but they don't want to offend her. We think we've worked out a compromise and I've sent Greg to Walla Walla to talk to her. His grandfather dated the old woman many years ago. I'm gambling that the connection might make Greg more influential than the rest of us."

Abby laughed softly. "You could use a spot of tea."

He tossed his gray tweed jacket on the hall tree. "You're right."

"Come. There's a kettle on the stove."

As Stephen settled into a chair at the kitchen table, Abby couldn't help but think how lucky a woman would be to have a man like Stephen Kraft coming home to her every night.

"I've told you about my day. How about yours?" he asked, crossing one long leg over the other.

For a moment, she avoided his eyes, fearful he might see in hers the attraction she felt toward him. "It was mostly lights and Christmas music. I took Daphne and Peter to the mall."

"Did they wear you out?"

"They did try to go off in all directions at once," she said, setting his tea in front of him. "But I found their excitement contagious. I rather got in the spirit of things myself."

"Did you sit on Santa's lap?" he asked coyly.

She cast him a wary look, then sat across from him. From the kitchen, she could see the children as they played in the next room with a basket of pinecones. The cat batted one back and forth. "I didn't, and neither did Peter. He thought he was much too grown up. But Daphne did."

"Did she talk his boots off?"

"They were cowboy boots, actually, but she seemed not to notice the discrepancy. No, her Christmas list was very short." At the moment the words came off her lips, she almost regretted having said them.

He glanced over his shoulder at the children and lowered his voice. "Perhaps you can drop the real Santa a hint."

Abby took a sip of tea. "She'd like a dollhouse, and . . ." She set down her cup and took a deep breath. "She asked for a mommy."

His chest heaved as he ran a hand over his jaw. "Uh-oh. Not again."

There was a beat of silence. Abby took another sip from her cup. For a moment, she didn't know what to say. "Perhaps she's just going through a phase."

"Perhaps not," he said, gazing at her intently. Her blood raced like it always did whenever he looked at her that way. "I'm just concerned that the older she gets, the more she'll feel the loss," he added.

"She has you. You can't be mother and father, but you're quite extraordinary," Abby said.

He reached across the table and put his hand over hers. He smiled softly. Her heart jumped.

"Thanks, Abby. A word of encouragement is always appreciated."

"Everyone could use one now and then," she said, struggling to ignore the heat of his hand on hers.

"Well," he said, leaning back in his chair. He folded his arms across his chest. "I meant to tell you that I was trying to arrange for you to meet Greg before the ball, but now he's off to Walla Walla. From there, he has to go to San Francisco for his sister's wedding. He'll be back in Seattle barely in time for the ball. I'm sorry, but it seems like I've gotten you into sort of a blind date. I wanted you two to meet before then."

Abby laughed. "I wouldn't be doing this, you know, if I didn't trust you."

"If I'm to understand you correctly, you didn't say you liked me. You just said that you trust me."

Abby offered him a cryptic smile, but said nothing. In the silence, she could almost hear the throbbing of her pulse. In the beginning, she didn't have to pretend she didn't like him. Now, life with Stephen had turned into a charade.

"Kendall brought the dress over today," she said finally. "It's beautiful."

"Good," he said. "I knew she'd come through."

While Stephen played with the children, Abby prepared a meal of fettucini, a salad, garlic bread, and baked apples. She thought of the ball, not with the reservation that she'd felt earlier, but with a glimmer of anticipation. Her world was too small, built around a man and two children to whom she was becoming dangerously attached. Perspective was what she needed. A night of dancing in the arms of a handsome stranger just might help her see life more clearly.

After supper, Abby noticed that Stephen appeared more tired than usual as he sat in the living room leafing through an architecture magazine. Daphne and Peter could be heard chattering in the kitchen.

"I can take the children upstairs if you'd like some quiet time to yourself," she offered.

Before he could answer, Peter bounded into the room. "Daddy, come see what I made."

Daphne came running after him and crawled into her father's lap. Smiling, Stephen turned to Abby with a shrug of feigned resignation. "Let's go see."

Abby followed them into the kitchen. On the long pine table Peter had constructed a cabin of play logs. With it were an outbuilding and a fence.

Stephen walked around the table, stroking his chin in an exaggerated expression of appraisal. His face suddenly brightened and he tousled the child's hair. "Good work, my man."

Peter beamed.

Not to be outdone again, Daphne produced her hourglass-shaped doll with the billowing hair. This time, the doll was outfitted in a red formal. "She's going to the ball," she said.

Stephen smiled. "I wouldn't have guessed."

"Daddy, would you teach me how to dance?" she asked.

Stephen, his face etched with fatigue, hedged for a moment. "Maybe some . . ."

"Please?" she asked, standing on her toes.

"All right," he said, "but this is going to be a very short lesson. Daddy's tired."

He took her by the hand and led her into the living room. He paused only long enough to turn on the stereo. "Madame Butterfly," which Abby had left in the machine, had begun to play. Stephen looked at Abby and winced.

"I'll get something else," she said.

"Never mind," he said. "It will do."

Stephen lifted Daphne and set her feet down on top of his shoes. Then he began to take small steps to the rhythm of the music. Daphne giggled.

Abby took Peter's hands and led him to the center of the room. She swayed gently to the music while he took clumsy sidesteps. Her eye caught Stephen's as they danced around each other. His eyes sparkled. Abby's heart kicked.

This moment, with its backdrop of violins and giggling

children, would stay in her memory forever. But would Daphne and Peter remember her? Would they fade out of her life like a passing season? She stopped dancing.

"Something wrong?" Stephen asked.

"Nothing," she said, feigning a smile. But inside, she wasn't smiling at all.

Abby made last-minute preparations for Mrs. Bybee. There were snacks in the refrigerator and she'd managed to find a video of a children's show that was popular in Europe. She scratched out a note about that and several other things.

Stephen laughed as she bustled about.

"What's so funny?" she asked. She placed her hands on her hips.

"You're acting as if they're your children and you're turning them over to a baby-sitter for the first time."

She felt herself blush. "Are you proposing that I leave them with scarcely a crumb to eat?"

She caught a glint of humor in his eyes. "I'm proposing that you relax a bit. The cabinets are full. Mrs. Bybee knows how to make a snack."

Abby shot him a look of annoyance. "Then what do you propose that I do instead?"

"Take a bubble bath. Polish your nails. Do whatever women do before a night of dancing."

"I don't have any idea what women do before a night of dancing," she said.

He held up his hands in mock defense. "Just a suggestion. Let me know if you need me. I'll be with the children."

Abby sighed. The truth was that she was too nervous to sit still. She'd already set out her black patent pumps. The dress had been laid out on the bed since early that morning.

It had fit beautifully. It gently followed her curves, then in a graceful sweep, fell to her toes. The night before, after Stephen and the children had gone to bed, Abby had stood before the full-length mirror in her room studying her reflection. The black taffeta had brought out the rich highlights in her dark hair, the golden tones of her skin, and the cool green of her eyes. It was as right for her as if she'd picked it out herself.

She stepped into the sunroom where Stephen was gazing out onto the patio as the children looked at books. His shoulders, broad and square, were silhouetted against the light. His hands were thrust deeply into his pockets.

"Stephen?"

He turned. She was surprised to find his expression vaguely troubled.

"I just want you to know I appreciate your thoughtfulness," she said. "I—I've never been to a ball before. I'm looking forward to it."

A slow smile that made her heart flutter spread across his face. "I'm pleased," he said.

On Saturday, Abby awoke in a nervous twitter. She spent the morning taking a leisurely shower and styling her hair while Stephen watched the children. Shortly before noon, everything seemed in order when the telephone rang.

Stephen took the call in the kitchen while Abby fed the cat. She couldn't help but overhear.

"What?" There was a ring of alarm in his voice.

Abby tensed as she detected increasing dismay in his tone.

"I'll get Abby," he said.

She looked up and saw that his expression was troubled.

"What is it?" she asked, her chest tightening.

"It's Greg calling from San Francisco. He's injured his knee."

"Oh, no," she said, feeling a twinge of weakness.

"He'd like to talk to you."

Her hand trembled slightly as she picked up the receiver. "Greg, it's Abby. I'm terribly sorry."

"Hello, Abby." His voice was low and gentle. She liked the sound of it. "I was so much looking forward to meeting you tonight. Stephen is always saying nice things about you. Now I've injured my leg and I can't make it back to Seattle in time for the ball. In fact, I even missed my sister's wedding reception."

"Never mind about me," she said, struggling to keep the disappointment out of her voice. "Tell me what happened."

"I was getting into my car to go to my sister's wedding reception when an elderly man suddenly backed up. His car knocked me to the ground and the rest is history. The doctors have patched me up. I'm going to have to stay here with my parents a few days. I called the first chance I got."

"I'm terribly sorry, but please don't worry about me," she said. "Just get better."

When Abby hung up, she put on a brave smile, but her heart felt leaden.

"It's a shame about Greg," Abby said, finding Stephen pacing back and forth in the sunroom. "But the bright side is that we won't have to trouble Mrs. Bybee."

He stopped pacing, then looked at her in that clear and direct way of his. "Abby, I wanted so much for you to have a nice night out."

She swallowed her disappointment. "Please don't let that stand in the way of your having a lovely evening."

"I'll make it up to you," he said, taking her hand in his

and giving it a gentle squeeze. Her heart fluttered. "I guess I should call Mrs. Bybee."

As Stephen disappeared into the kitchen, Peter got up and put his arms around her waist. "Abby, I'll take you to that dance."

A lump rose to her throat as she pressed the boy's head against her midriff. "Peter, that's so sweet of you." She bent down, kissed the top of his head, and looked into his eyes. They were the same color as his father's. In the background, she heard Stephen hang up the phone. "Let's make the best of it, Peter. Let's just stay here and have a lovely evening ourselves. We can make some jammy dodgers."

"Does that require any power tools?" She turned to find Stephen in the doorway looking slightly bemused.

"I realize British cooking suffers from a poor reputation," she said, "but all it takes is a wooden spoon, not a power saw."

"What is it?" he said.

"It's a biscuit—I mean, a cookie," she said, slightly miffed.

"Save some for me."

"I'll sweep up a few crumbs."

With considerable mess, Abby involved the children in cookie-making and even let them stay up a bit past their bedtime. After she tucked them in, she caught sight of the black ball gown still carefully laid out on her bed. It wasn't until then that an eerie sense of loneliness began to envelop her.

Abby turned on some soft music and curled up on the sofa with a magazine. It was nearly ten o'clock but she was too restless to go to bed. As she turned through the pages, her thoughts skipped through the events of the day, then settled on Stephen. In his tuxedo, he'd looked so extraordinarily handsome that it had taken all her restraint to keep from staring at him. She tried to read, but it was his image that she saw on the pages. It was as pleasant as it was troubling.

Just as she got up to make herself a cup of tea, she saw a flash of lights in the driveway. She glanced through the window to see the silhouette of the Volvo. Her heart skipped in surprise. She glanced at her watch. It was just barely ten. She hadn't been expecting Stephen until midnight.

Before she could get to the door, Stephen and Kendall entered. Kendall was dressed in a clinging ice-blue gown shimmering with beadwork. It matched her eyes, which at this moment were also cool. Her lips were firmly set. Abby, wearing Mrs. Bybee's old brown chenille robe, sensed a sudden tension in the air.

"You're early," she said, self-consciously tightening her sash. "Is everything all right?"

"Get dressed, Abby," Stephen said, his expression unreadable. "We're going to the ball."

Her pulse leaped with surprise. "But Stephen . . ."

"Don't worry about the children. Kendall will sit with them for a while."

Abby looked at Kendall in disbelief.

Kendall nodded stiffly.

Abby was speechless for a moment. "You really don't need to . . ."

"Take off that abominable robe and get dressed," Stephen said firmly, "before my car turns into a pumpkin."

"Of course," she said. She lifted her hem slightly and quickly tripped up the stairs.

Her hands trembled as she hurriedly applied makeup. Her thoughts were scrambled. Why would Stephen do this, especially when Kendall didn't seem pleased with the idea? She wanted to go and to stay home at the same time.

She slipped into the black taffeta dress and zipped it with a struggle. She fluffed the bow at the shoulder, then quickly combed her straight hair. She slipped on a pair of tiny diamond earrings that had belonged to her mother and quickly checked her image in the mirror. The transformation from brown robe to black evening gown was a significant one, even she had to admit.

Her heart racing, she descended the stairs and almost shyly entered the living room. Stephen, standing by the fireplace, turned. His lips parted. His eyes widened.

Abby, unused to such intense scrutiny, felt a blushing heat on her cheeks. "Would you rather I put Mrs. Bybee's robe back on?"

He took a deep breath, his nostrils flaring. "Not in the least." He turned to Kendall, who stood behind him looking miffed. "The dress is perfect for her. Don't you think so?"

"It's very becoming," she said tonelessly.

Stephen kissed Kendall's cheek. "Thanks for sitting with the children," he said. "We'll be back in an hour or so."

It wasn't until Abby got outside that she realized she was without a wrap. The evening chill had raised goose bumps over her bare arms and shoulders. Stephen took off the jacket to his tuxedo and draped it over her shoulders. "There," he said as they got into the car.

The fabric of her gown rustled as she slid onto the leather seat. "Stephen," she said, turning toward him, "you're very kind to think of me, but you really don't have to do all this. I don't want to spoil the evening for Kendall."

His eyes glittered in the lamplight. "Don't argue, and don't worry about Kendall. She just isn't used to some of my spur-of-the-moment decisions. Save your energy for dancing.''

The light cast a golden glow over his face. She'd never seen him look so handsome. His tucked shirt was crisp and white, his black bow tie slightly crooked. For a moment, she had the impulse to reach over and straighten it. Instead, she leaned back and tried to savor the moment.

For the first few blocks, they traveled in silence. How grand it would be if he were taking her to the ball simply because he wanted to be with her. But she knew better. He was doing this out of kindness, because he felt a little sorry for her. She touched the satiny lapel of his jacket and stifled a sigh.

"Do you believe in ghosts?" he asked.

Puzzled, Abby turned to him. "Why, did one just fly over the bonnet?"

"Bonnet?"

"You know, the hood."

He chuckled softly. "You English."

"You Americans," she retorted. "You haven't spoken English in years."

Stephen cast her a look of amusement, then slowed the car. On the right was a large park with an arched bridge. "There's a legend that if you stand by that bridge at a certain angle, you can see the ghost of a bride. The story is that she died in a carriage mishap on her way to her wedding."

"Have you ever seen her?"

"No, but some people swear they have seen a moving blur of white."

"Let's go have a look," she said impulsively.

Without answering, Stephen turned into the drive leading to the bridge and quickly parked. She eagerly got out and, lifting up the hem of her gown, briskly walked the few steps to the edge of the bridge. Stephen stood behind her and placed a hand on her bare shoulder. Her skin caught fire.

"Look to the other side of the bridge," he said, his lips close to her ear.

Abby gasped in amazement. White tendrils of mist, illuminated by a lamp, danced in the air. "I see her!"

Stephen laughed. "You see? Some people find images in clouds, others in fog."

"And now you've seen her, too," she said.

"So I have."

The ball was just a twist and a turn away down a narrow road leading through tall wrought-iron gates. At the end was an Italian Renaissance–style house that had been converted into an art museum.

"How lovely," Abby marveled.

"First the ghost," he said, "and now the castle."

The entry was a large expanse of imported Italian marble and beyond that a grand room with chandeliers and dozens of dancing couples. A string orchestra filled the air with the lilting strains of a waltz.

Before she could comprehend it all, Stephen's arm slipped around her waist and he swept her onto the ballroom floor in a motion that almost took her breath away. His steps were sure, practiced and smooth.

"I forgot to ask," he said coyly. "May I have this dance?"

"It's too late to say no. And don't step on my right toe. I stubbed it yesterday."

His eyes contained a glint of mischief. "Don't tempt me."

He pulled her closer and her heart seemed to take on

wings. His palm pulsed against her hand and his cheek, for one fleeting moment, brushed softly against her temple. Then the music stopped. Abby, struggling to restrain her runaway heart, was relieved.

They sipped punch and sampled hors d'oeuvres. They chatted with his friends and a half hour vanished. "The children," she whispered guiltily.

He laughed softly. "They're in good hands. Come, let me step on your toes some more."

They danced to a silky rendition of "Yesterday," then to "A Whiter Shade of Pale." She felt so right in his arms, but she knew that her feelings, which had been beating against the inside of her chest with an intensity she couldn't ignore, were all wrong.

Stephen pulled away for a moment. "I almost hate to tell Greg what he's missed."

"Tell him the orchestra was out of tune and the punch was sour."

"And what should I tell him about you?"

"I'll leave that up to your imagination."

He smiled wryly. "Perhaps a little fresh air would stimulate my thinking."

He led her through a set of open terrace doors. The stars twinkled through a small clearing in the Seattle sky. The opening notes of "Moon River" floated outside. "One of my favorites," he said, taking her hand and slipping his arm around her waist. "Indulge me."

The distance between them closed and the cool night air seemed to heat. His nearness was intoxicating as he guided her along the tiled floor. The music stopped much too soon, but for an instant after the last note had sounded, Stephen had kept her in his arms, his cheek pressed against her hair. Her heart beat wildly against his chest.

Then he pulled away, holding her at arm's length. He looked into her eyes. Unable to avoid his any longer, she lost herself in the depths of their pale intensity. And it was in that instant, she realized with horror, that she had given herself away.

Chapter Nine

They rode home from the ball in a silence that was almost palpable. A fine mist speckled the windshield as Stephen, his clean, square profile etched into the darkness by passing lights, watched the road with what seemed to Abby to be an inordinate amount of concentration.

He knows, she thought, her heart sinking to her toes. *When a woman loses herself in his eyes, a man has to know.*

She swallowed hard, tasting bitter remorse. It was the heated touch of his strong fingers at her waist, the soft brush of his jaw against her cheek, and the sure way in which he moved that toppled her defenses. All it took was his penetrating gray gaze to crack the safe in which she had guarded her feelings.

And what were those feelings? Attraction, to be certain. But there was something deeper, something she didn't want to explore, especially now. All she knew was that her heart fluttered at the sound of his voice, at the anticipation of his coming home. And now he probably knew, despite her promise that it would never happen, that she was attracted

119

to him. She was a professional. She wasn't even supposed to get emotionally attached to the children.

She took a deep, cleansing breath and sat up straight.

"A penny for your thoughts," he said.

"They'd be hardly worth it," she said, trying hard to sound composed. The taffeta of her gown rustled.

He cast her a glance of wry skepticism. "Well, then, I'll tell you what I'm thinking. I think Peter may have a bit of a crush on you."

Abby gave a short laugh of surprise. "But he's just a little boy."

"Little boys can have big hearts."

"I'm sure it's just a phase," she said. "Besides, it would never work out. All we have in common is our love of dinosaurs."

Stephen pulled under the large elm shading the driveway and parked the car. He placed his arm on the back of the seat and turned toward her. His fingers were very close to her shoulder. "A man can always hope," he said, smiling crookedly.

She grinned, then a cloud seemed to hover over her.

"Something wrong?" he asked.

"Oh, Stephen," she said. "I'm going to miss both of the children so much." She took a deep breath to settle her leaping emotions. "I shouldn't have gone to the ball. Violin music always turns me into putty."

His bottom lip jutted out in perplexity.

"I mean . . ." She gave a shrug of frustration. "It was a lovely evening. Thank you."

Then she bent over and gave him a chaste and sisterly kiss on the cheek. Her lips burned.

Stephen's eyes widened. "You're welcome, Abby."

When they entered the house, they found Kendall chatting on the telephone in the kitchen. She said a quick "good-bye" and hung up.

"Stephen, darling," she said, taking both of his hands in hers. She kissed him lightly on the lips.

Abby's stomach tightened.

"Hello, Abby," Kendall said with a stiff smile. "You had a nice time?"

"Very," she said. "And thank you once again for letting me wear this lovely dress." Abby couldn't help but notice that she continued to hold Stephen's hands.

"You're quite welcome," Kendall said sweetly. She turned to Stephen. "I was just chatting with Brooke Westminster. They'd like us for dinner next week. Saturday, to be precise. It's a holiday affair."

"Just the sort of thing you love," he said, turning to Abby with a wink.

Abby forced a smile as Kendall straightened his tie. It had been something Abby had been longing to do all night.

"Any peeps out of the children?" Stephen asked.

"Not a sound," Kendall said.

"Abby can take over now. Shall we go back to the ball?"

"I'd love to," she said.

After hasty good-byes, Abby heard the front door close and a lonely silence fell over the house.

The next morning, Abby threw on an old white thermal undershirt, an especially baggy red plaid flannel jumper that grazed her ankles, black tights, and her old Doc Martens. She wore no makeup.

The night before, she'd said violin music had made her lose her senses. That had been her excuse for ogling him like a lovesick schoolgirl when he'd looked into her eyes.

Then she had to go kiss him on the cheek. It seemed like a sisterly gesture at the time, but now she saw it as a blunder. Nannies could kiss their charges, but not their charges' fathers.

She studied herself critically in the mirror, crossing her arms over her chest. He couldn't get the wrong idea about her today, not when she chose to look like a disheveled teenager.

She dressed the children and fed them scrambled eggs, toast, and cocoa. She told them about the ball. Peter declared that he would never get hit by a car like Greg because he always looked both ways before crossing the street. But a half hour went by and Stephen still hadn't come down for breakfast. There had been no sign of him except for a pair of shiny black oxfords by the front door. It must have been quite late when he came home, she thought. She hadn't heard a sound.

She tried to crowd out memories of the ball by thinking of English heather, the sea crashing onto the cliffs of Dover, and browsing in the quaint shops of London, but images of Stephen kept coming back to her.

She settled the children down for play and picked up Boom, who was growing into a very handsome cat. He tickled her face with his whiskers, then went scampering off after the children. She heaved a little sigh. She was even going to miss the kitten.

She had just finished clearing the table when Daphne came back into the kitchen holding a naked doll. "I can't find her cowgirl outfit," she said, a pout playing on her bottom lip.

"Did you look in your room?" Abby asked.

The little girl nodded.

"Let's go look again," Abby said. "Things have been known to find their way under the bed or some such place."

Abby followed the child upstairs, placing her finger at her lips to indicate they mustn't disturb Stephen. She entered Daphne's room and checked the toy box, without success. She looked under the bed and under and around the rest of the furniture. Then she went back to the toy box and pulled it out from the wall. Behind it was not only the cowgirl outfit, but a missing coloring book.

Pleased, Daphne went bouncing down the stairs while Abby paused to open a window slightly. As she stepped into the hall to go back downstairs, she turned to find Stephen coming down the hall carrying a towel. He wore the bottom half of a pair of pale-blue pajamas. Their eyes met in a flash of mutual surprise.

"Close your mouth before a moth flies in," he said teasingly.

Abby felt her color deepen. "Pardon me, I was just helping Daphne find something." She could barely keep her eyes off the sculpted planes of his broad chest. It was covered by a film of curling brown hair.

A small dimple appeared in his unshaven cheek. "It's quite all right."

Her heart beating rapidly, Abby quickly descended the stairs. She didn't need any more tantalizing images of Stephen Kraft to haunt her imagination. Her mouth had been open. How could she have been so transparent?

She looked in on Peter and Daphne, whose doll now bore a resemblance to Annie Oakley. Distractedly, she played with them for a few moments. Then she went to the living room to put on some music to quell her restlessness. She fumbled through her opera collection. She put on

Madame Butterfly, knowing Stephen disliked it. She smiled mischievously. She felt better already.

She went to the kitchen, put two eggs in a saucepan, and covered them with water. He liked three-minute eggs. Once the water began to boil, she set the timer for ten. He liked his toast light. She turned the toaster setting to dark. She sat at the kitchen table, arms folded across her chest, fingers tapping nervously, and waited.

A few long moments later, Stephen entered the kitchen singing along to the strains of the music. His rich baritone was surprisingly clear and polished.

She looked at him in surprise.

"You're making an opera convert out of me, Abby," he said. His hair was damp, his freshly shaven face rosy. He wore a pair of corduroys and his old cardigan over a faded denim shirt. "But I wouldn't want the guys at the office to know."

She cast him an exaggerated look of annoyance. "Your secret is safe with me."

Stephen offered her a playful smile, then followed the sounds of the children's voices in the sunroom.

Abby sighed. Did he have to turn good-humored on her? And did he have to look so good at the same time?

She placed the egg in an egg cup and plopped it on the table so firmly that the egg gave a little bounce of protest. She buttered the toast and sliced it diagonally, noting with satisfaction the charred edges of the crust. She set the plate of toast on the table along with a lukewarm glass of orange juice. She'd show him how much she cared.

She stepped into the sunroom where she found him helping Peter construct another log house. "Your breakfast is ready," she said cheerfully.

A moment later, Stephen took his place at the kitchen

table. She set down a steaming cup of tea and sat next to him. He took a sip of juice, eyeing her over the rim of his glass.

"You look interesting today, Abby," he said.

She smiled. "Is that a tactful way of saying 'strange'?"

"Not at all," he said. "You've got a certain—well, let's say 'style.' "

She looked at him warily. "Eat your breakfast," she said.

He responded with the barest of smiles. She took a quick breath of frustration. He wasn't supposed to like what she was wearing.

Abby watched over the rim of her teacup as Stephen tapped on the shell of his egg with his spoon. "Nothing quite like a good soft-boiled egg," he said, peeling part of the shell gently away. He scooped at the egg, but the pressure wasn't enough to penetrate the white. He pushed harder while Abby pretended to busy herself by adding lemon to her tea. Finally, he lifted the egg out of the cup, finished peeling it, and sliced it in half.

"Of course, hard-boiled is nice for a change," he said with a glitter of amusement in his eyes.

Abby smiled weakly. Did he have to start being so congenial? "Shall I get more butter for your toast?" she asked.

Stephen picked up a triangle of bread, not seeming to notice that it looked as if it had been held over a blowtorch. "It's fine the way it is," he said with a shrug of nonchalance.

Abby gulped the remainder of her tea and got up. She straightened things on the counter that needed straightening and straightened things that didn't. Her heart beat rapidly. He was no longer the brooding, hard-to-please man she'd met when she'd first arrived. He'd turned impossibly congenial. And to make matters worse, the change in his disposition was probably due to his increasing interest in Kendall. Perhaps he was too absorbed in her to worry about how Abby might feel about him. How foolish of her to think he might be concerned about it. Suddenly, she felt a strong need to get out of the house.

She turned, surprised to notice that Stephen was finishing off the last piece of toast. "What if I take the children for a walk?" she asked.

He got up and turned toward her, touching the corners of his mouth with a napkin. "That would be nice," he said. "I have a drawing that I need to finish—the redesign of Mrs. Bentley's pink hospital wing. Greg was able to make her see the light."

Peter was anxious to see how the excavation was proceeding for the new school, so they made the six-block walk in no time at all. The hole was vast and considerably deeper than before. It was protected by a fencing of orange net. Peter stared at it in rapt fascination.

"Where do you suppose they took the dirt?" he asked.

"I don't know," Abby replied.

"What if it had dinosaur bones in it?"

Abby laughed softly. "I have a hunch there weren't any."

"Could there be some down there?" he asked, pointing at the hole.

"Yes, but it's very unlikely."

"I'd sure like to find one," he said wistfully. "I'd put it in my room."

"Come on, little archaeologist," she said, giving his hand a tug. "It's time to go home."

* * *

Abby had the afternoon off. The free time was especially appreciated now because she wanted to distance herself from Stephen. She went to an art gallery, but instead of the pictures, she saw his dimpled chin and sardonic smile. She went to a mall where she was surrounded by a flurry of Christmas shoppers. Carols filled the air, but between the notes, she heard the sound of his voice.

She bought a gaily colored silk scarf for Aunt Margo and a fashion magazine and a small box of chocolates for herself. Chocolates, she reasoned, always lifted her spirits. She ate two and felt better. She vowed to be strong. In a month, she'd be back in England. She would concentrate on what awaited her there, not what she was leaving behind.

She wasn't terribly hungry, but to delay returning home, she stopped for a supper of pizza and salad. She lingered over her food and took a long route home, but when she arrived at the Krafts', the house was empty except for Boom. She gave him a hug and went to the kitchen. On the refrigerator was a note printed in Stephen's precise hand: *Abby, we've gone to Kendall's. Be back by eight.*

Before she had time to finish a cup of tea, she heard the front door open.

"Abby!" Daphne called.

Abby hurried to the front entry. Stephen was helping Peter out of his coat, but Daphne was tearing toward the living room. Her mittens, which Abby had attached to her sleeves with ribbons, flapped. "Guess what we got!"

Abby lifted the little girl into her arms. "What is it, pumpkin?"

"A Christmas tree!" Peter interjected.

Daphne frowned. "I wanted to tell her first."

Stephen, his face reddened by the cold, strode into the

living room. Yet his expression didn't mirror the children's excitement. His brow was crinkled slightly, his mouth firmly set. He glanced at Abby only briefly. "I left it in the garage," he said, turning his attention toward Peter. "Tomorrow night, we can do the trimming, but right now it's time for you two to get ready for bed."

"Oh, Dad," Peter pleaded, "can we at least bring the tree in the house tonight?"

Stephen shook his head. "Later, son," he repeated.

Daphne stuck out her bottom lip in an exaggerated pout.

Abby was acutely aware of the fact that Stephen hadn't yet greeted her. It was almost as if she weren't there.

"Abby," he said finally, "I'll get the children to bed."

Daphne threw her arms around Abby's thighs. "Good night, Abby."

"Good night, love," she said, bending over and kissing the little girl's golden curls.

Peter held out his arms to her and kissed her cheek.

"Sweet dreams," she said, placing a kiss on his forehead. She looked up to find Stephen looking at her intently. Her heart gave a kick.

"I'll be back down shortly," he said.

Abby, her heart tripping, poured herself another cup of tea and curled up on the sofa. But she couldn't relax. Upstairs, there was a certain heaviness to the sound of Stephen's footsteps. Something was wrong. She could sense it.

Lost in thought, she picked up her cup. Her tea had turned cold. Then she heard footsteps on the staircase and Stephen entered the room.

"All tucked in," he said with a strained smile.

"Thank you," she said.

He shook his head. "If anything, I should be thanking you."

"I'm not sure what you mean." His presence made her blood race.

"You give a lot of yourself. You mean a lot to . . . to the children." His normally smooth and confident voice faltered for an instant.

She managed a smile despite the little ache under her heart. "They mean a lot to me as well."

He ran a hand through his hair and paced nervously over the carpet.

"Stephen, can I get you some tea?" she asked. "You seem as if something is troubling you."

He took a deep breath. "I'm sorry, Abby," he said. "It's just that I have a lot on my mind. I'll pass on the tea, but why don't you come down to the basement with me? I'd like to show you something."

She followed him down a stairway leading off the kitchen. He took her to a door at the end of the basement, one that she had assumed belonged to a storage room. He unlocked it and stepped inside. A flood of fluorescent light lit up the room. Inside was a woodworking shop. It smelled of sawdust.

"I keep the door locked because of the children," he said. He stood by what appeared to be an architectural model made of plywood. Its curves and turret suggested something Victorian. He turned it to show the open rooms on the other side. "It's Daphne's Christmas present."

"Oh, Stephen," Abby marveled. "It's the dollhouse she wanted, and you're making it yourself."

"For better or worse," he said with a grin. He reached for a rolled-up piece of drafting paper and unfurled it. On it was a sketch of a Victorian house with shutters and a wraparound porch. "I could use a consultant." For the first time, Abby noticed that he had a Band-Aid on his thumb.

"You cut yourself?"

"Just a nick with a saw."

"Count your fingers before you leave to make sure you have the same number you came in with."

"I intend to, my dear one," he said, his eyes glittering.

She tried to ignore the term of endearment, but it kept echoing through her head. "What's this about needing a consultant?" she asked after an awkward pause.

"Perhaps you might tell me what Daphne's latest favorite color is."

"It's still pink," she answered quickly.

The corners of his mouth tipped into a smile. "A pink house it is, then."

"Green shutters and white trim would be nice," she offered. "Try dark gray for the roof."

"Any other ideas?" He laid the plans down and leaned against the counter with his arms folded. "I've got to do something about the rooms, and I'm no interior decorator. I know this is not in your job description, but . . . could you do the inside?" He looked at her beseechingly. It was a look that threatened to make her heart melt like wax.

"For Daphne, I will," she said.

He gave her a chiding look. "What about me? I was getting my hopes up that it might even be possible for you to like me, too."

"Hope springs eternal," she said dryly.

"I wasn't that bad of a dancer, was I? What's wrong, did you count your toes after the ball and come up short?"

"You're getting frisky," she said. "You must be feeling better."

He responded with a tentative smile. "Maybe."

"Let's get back to the house," she said. "I'll get some wallpaper scraps and lace for the curtains. Some bits of fabric will do nicely for the rugs. Of course, we should get the furniture first."

"If you trust my taste, I'll do that on my way home from the office tomorrow. There's a craft store nearby."

"It's settled then," Abby said.

"Good," he said, touching her elbow. "Thank you, Abby."

"You're welcome," she said, turning to go. Being near him was almost intoxicating. She wanted to get away.

"Don't go," he said.

Her heart skipped in surprise as she turned to face him. His eyes were dark and penetrating. "I—I thought you might enjoy seeing the dollhouse take shape." There was an undertone to his voice that hinted of loneliness.

"Of course," she said.

She watched in silence as he measured a small piece of wood that was to become the front porch. He cut the piece with skill and when he finished, it perfectly fit the contours of the front of the house. Then he cut the supporting pieces.

"Did I ever tell you about the last Christmas that Diane and I had together?" he asked, breaking the silence.

She looked at him in surprise. "No, you didn't."

"The children were asleep. It was Christmas Eve and we'd just put the presents under the tree. We were sitting on the sofa in the dark, watching the tree lights twinkle and drinking hot chocolate, when Diane said, 'Sometimes I think our life together is too good to be true.' It was almost prophetic what she was saying. I didn't want to talk about it, but she seemed oddly comfortable with it. She talked of how she would want her parents involved in the children's upbringing and that she wanted Kendall to play a strong role. She made me promise that I would see to that.

"Of course, I saw no reason for such a promise, but it seemed to put her at ease."

Abby instinctively placed her hand on Stephen's arm. "Stephen, I know Christmas must be hard for you."

He placed a hand over hers, generating a fire that leapt at her heart. She wanted to pull him into her arms like she did one of the children when they needed her comfort, but her instincts toward their father were far from just motherly.

He squeezed her hand, then pulled away. "I am adjusting to Diane's death. The past few months have been much better. I'm moving on, Abby. Life is beginning to look good to me again."

She took a deep breath. "That's wonderful. That's the way Diane would have wanted it."

"I know," he said softly, absently toying with a piece of wood. "It's not that my life is no longer complicated. There are still things I'm wrestling with, but I've crossed a bridge. I have to tell you, Abby, that your own special brand of sunshine around this house has been appreciated. It hasn't gone without notice."

Her heart jumped, then faltered. If only he knew how much she was going to miss him and the children. "I was simply doing my job," she said, struggling to hide her feelings behind the shield of duty.

"When it comes to the children, I think it was more than that," he said. "I just want you to know that you shouldn't worry about us after you leave."

She looked into his eyes, barely able to keep her composure. "Peter and Daphne won't be easy to forget."

"I know. So there's something I should tell you, Abby. Kendall and I will give them the love and support they need. We stayed up very late talking about it. To be specific, Kendall and I are talking about marriage."

Chapter Ten

Abby's heart seemed to plummet to her toes. The room turned so still that even the clock on the workshop wall seemed to stop. She struggled desperately to find the poise, grace, and composure that the moment demanded.

"I hope you find the happiness you deserve," she said after an eternity seemed to elapse. Her voice was soft and slightly unsteady.

A slightly melancholy grin appeared on his lips. "Thank you, Abby. That's very kind of you."

"You have indeed crossed a bridge," she said with a lightness she didn't feel.

"Kendall and I think it's the right thing to do, especially for the children," he said, searching her eyes. "They need a mother. I'm sure you'll agree."

"Yes," she said quietly.

"Perhaps someday when you're back in England and you see some little girl with wild blond curls or a little boy with a passion for books and adventure, you'll be reminded of Peter and Daphne. And I hope you'll be secure in the knowledge that a void in their lives will have been, at least in some measure, filled.''

She pushed down the lump rising in her throat. ''I'll always know that you have their best interests at heart.''

''Always,'' he said, his eyes clear, gray pools. She knew she'd always remember the way he looked at this moment, his hair with a golden sheen and the light playing over the angles of his face. She wanted to turn and run, to let the tears flow, tears she had no right to cry. But she summoned all the will she could muster and stood before him, straightening her spine in defiance of her own feelings.

''Do the children know yet?'' she asked.

''I'm going to take it slowly and let them get used to the idea,'' he said. ''I'm not going to tell them right away.''

''Perhaps that's wise,'' she said with an ache inside.

One corner of his mouth quirked in a half smile. ''Father doesn't always know best. All I can do is try.''

''Nanny doesn't always have the answers either,'' she said. The ache inside her persisted.

''Well, then, let's get on with something simpler—the dollhouse,'' he said. ''I suppose you can keep a secret. I want to surprise Daphne on Christmas morning.''

''Scout's honor,'' she said, holding up three unsteady fingers. But behind the fanciful facade, she was holding the biggest secret of all—that her heart was close to breaking.

Kendall breezed in the next evening with a take-charge attitude. The occasion was a tree-decorating party. Dressed in a hand-knit red sweater with a Christmas-tree design and buttons that looked like ornaments, she arrived with bags of potpourri, a eucalyptus wreath, Christmas carols on compact discs, cranberry- and bayberry-scented candles, and the first gifts to go under the tree.

Abby watched as Stephen, who had just gotten home moments before, greeted her with a quick kiss. Abby had been up half the previous night giving herself lessons in logic, telling herself that it was a waste of time to yearn for a man she could never have. Still, she ached every time she saw him touch Kendall.

"Hello, little angels," Kendall greeted, giving each child a hug. "I've got some little presents for you." She reached into a glossy red shopping bag and produced two gingerbread men. "Perhaps Abby can put them away until after supper."

"Hello, Kendall," Abby said, managing to affect a casualness in her voice that she didn't feel. "It was very thoughtful of you to bring them something."

Kendall was lovely with her blond hair restrained with a red velvet ribbon and her pale cheeks tinged with the cold. Yet her eyes held their familiar coolness. "It's a special occasion," she said. "It's the trimming of the Kraft family tree."

"Let's get started," Stephen said, the tone of his voice unreadable.

While Stephen and Peter went out to the garage to get the tree, Kendall surveyed the living room. "The candles would do nicely on the mantel with some greenery," Kendall said. "That is, if you don't mind moving those other things."

Abby glanced at the arrangement of Thanksgiving gourds she'd placed on a blanket of autumn leaves. "Of course," she said, gathering them up.

She'd had her own plans for the mantel. She was going to have the children do a series of bright holiday drawings, place them in inexpensive brass frames, and set them on a lace runner. As she gathered the gourds into a basket, Kendall began replacing them with what seemed to be dozens of fragrant white candles of all sizes and heights. Each came with a little brass saucer.

As Abby watched, feeling somewhat displaced, the front door opened. Stephen entered, dragging a large and shapely cedar. Peter followed. "Where shall we put it?" Stephen asked.

Kendall moved quickly to orchestrate the tree-raising. "How about here?" she asked, pointing to a corner.

Stephen pulled the trunk toward the corner, fastened on the stand, and carefully raised the tree. The point came a few inches short of the ceiling. The children looked at it in awe. Kendall slipped an arm around Stephen's waist. "It's perfect," she said, kissing his cheek. Abby felt an emptiness in her chest.

"You would think so," Stephen said. "You're not the one who had to transport it five miles from a tree farm and who got needles in your clothes."

"Scrooge," Kendall replied.

The doorbell rang. "It must be the caterer," Kendall said, rushing to answer it.

"Caterer?" Stephen asked. He turned to Abby with a puzzled expression on his face.

Abby smiled politely, feeling like a lone spectator in a grand, staged event. In a matter of seconds, several trays of food were being transported through the hallway and into the kitchen by two young men in black-and-white striped aprons and mock chefs' hats.

Kendall brought out all of the best china and silver and laid it alongside a table runner with appliquéd holly leaves. They ate from a selection of meats, imported cheeses, homemade breads, and soups while Kendall and Stephen talked of the Christmases of their childhood. There was wine for the adults and milk for the children.

Abby remained silent, busying herself with the children, cutting their meat and making sure the soup was sufficiently cool. Her own food was barely touched.

"Abby, tell a Christmas story about your childhood," Stephen said.

She'd felt so far removed from the festivities that she was almost startled at the mention of her name. She thought for a moment. "Well, there really was a Scrooge in my neighborhood." She directed her story toward the children. "His name was Mr. Applegate and he was a grouch of the first order. He didn't like children walking on his grass. He didn't like children making noise. He didn't like children roller-skating down his sidewalk. Children, he said, should be seen and not heard.

"Of course, we played jokes on him just because he was so cross with us just for being children. When I was eight, my parents punished me for squirting catsup on his shirts as they hung out on the line."

The children interrupted with giggles, Stephen grinned wryly, his eyes shining with interest, but Kendall looked at her, unsmiling. Abby shifted uncomfortably in her seat and continued.

"Then that Christmas, my mother said that I should get Mr. Applegate a gift. Of course, I protested. Why should I buy something for someone who didn't like children? But Mum insisted. We got him a little plum pudding and three nice hankies. I was relieved to get that over with until Mum dropped the news that I was to deliver the gift by myself. Of course, I was loath to do it, and to make matters worse, I had to dress up in my Sunday best. Then, on Christmas Eve, with very strict instructions from my parents, I went next door to Mr. Applegate's and rang the bell. My knees were shaking. When he opened the door and saw that it was I, his eyes turned as cold as icicles.

" 'What do you want, child?' he asked." Abby emulated his booming voice.

"I told him I wanted to wish him a merry Christmas. My voice was shaking and so was my hand when I gave him the gift. I was going by a script that Mum had made me memorize. I told him I hoped he enjoyed the gift. He seemed so stunned that all he could do was stare at it. Finally, I put it in his hand. Then I told him the hardest thing of all to say, that it was from me."

"And then what happened?" Peter asked.

"Mr. Applegate never scowled at me again. In fact, he was kinder toward all the neighborhood children."

"Tell us another story, Abby," Daphne said. There was a smear of soup on her cheek.

"Later, sweetheart," she said, reaching over to wipe Daphne's cheek. "It's almost time to decorate the tree."

At their father's cue, the children excused themselves and rushed toward the living room. Stephen rose. "Kendall and I will clean up later," he said. "Just enjoy watching the children. I wouldn't want you to think of me as Mr. Applegate."

"It's all right. You needn't worry about your shirts."

Stephen responded with a half smile, then ushered Kendall into the living room. The children were already elbows deep into a box of Christmas decorations. Abby felt a surge of excitement and sadness at the same time. Children gave her energy and hope, but the thought of leaving these two and their father made her heart feel as though it would crumple.

Kendall slipped a compact disc into the player, and "Silent Night" flowed softly through the room. The scent of the candles and the cedar wafted about and the children, unable to contain their excitement, began to hang decorations as far as they could reach on the tree. Abby gently warned them against pricking their fingers.

Abby looked up to find Stephen standing in the doorway gazing at her and the children. She was so taken by the raw sentimentality in his eyes that she dropped the wooden ornament she was holding.

"It's a good thing they're unbreakable, Miss Fumblefingers."

"Here, Santa," she said, handing him the wooden bell. "You do it. It's your tree."

"In due time. The top third is mine."

Abby turned her attention back toward the children for a few moments, studying the ornaments featuring pictures of Daphne and Peter as newborns. As she turned to get another decoration, she saw Kendall taking Stephen's hand and pulling him under a cluster of freshly hung mistletoe that dangled from a red ribbon in the living room doorway. Her arms slipped around his neck and their lips met. Something inside Abby's chest wrenched and she quickly turned away. "Deck the Halls" now played, but she felt anything but jolly.

She took a deep breath and ventured another glance toward Kendall and Stephen, relieved to find they were no longer embracing. She did her best to smile.

"I really should catch up on some of my work," she said. "Could you excuse me, please?"

Stephen's eyes sharpened. "Forget about work, Abby. It's almost Christmas."

"Unless I take care of the laundry, your children are going to be rumbling about in their birthday suits."

A corner of his mouth quirked upward. "All right, then, but join us again when you're finished."

Abby loaded the washing machine, then began to clear the dining room table despite Stephen's offer to do it. It was her only way to deal with the anxiety that raced through her veins like little soldiers carrying spears.

The spirited voices of the children and occasional laughter from Stephen and Kendall carried into the kitchen. She fed and played with the cat, then went upstairs to straighten the children's rooms. All the time, she reminded herself of her place in the Kraft household—that of a nanny, and a temporary one at that.

She went nervously from one task to another, turning down the children's beds and laying out their nightclothes. Suddenly, she heard footsteps in the hallway. She stepped out of Daphne's room to find Stephen.

"Come see the tree," he said, taking her by the elbow. "We're going to switch on the lights."

His grasp on her arm was gentle, but firm. He swept her down the steps so fast that her feet barely seemed to touch the treads.

Daphne and Peter were bouncing up and down with excitement. "Hurry, Abby," Peter cried.

Kendall waited, exhibiting her characteristically cool elegance.

Stephen positioned Abby in front of the tree, which was now covered with an eclectic collection of stars, angels, toys, and tinsel. A large gold star now teetered on top.

"Lovely," Abby said in a near whisper.

"Just wait," Stephen said. He clicked a switch and the cedar was aglow with twinkling little golden lights. There was a rush of adult applause and squeals from the children.

Kendall placed the first gifts under the tree, three red-ribboned boxes of assorted sizes. "Now, you must wait until Christmas to open them," she instructed.

"Where's Abby's present?" Daphne asked.

There was a beat of silence as Kendall's delicate coloring deepened.

"We usually only give gifts to family members or people we know very well," Abby interjected in an attempt to salvage the moment. She felt a slight throb of embarrassment.

Kendall's expression softened and she glanced at Abby with a hint of gratitude. "I've only just begun my Christmas shopping," she said.

Daphne looked somewhat appeased.

"Darlings, I really must rush," Kendall said. "I have a board meeting in the morning and a charity bazaar in the afternoon. I'll barely have time for a breath."

She positioned each child under the mistletoe for a kiss, then said good night to Stephen with a chaste touch of her lips to his. He followed her to the door, then stepped outside with her.

"It's time for bed," Abby told the children. "You must be tired after decorating such a lovely tree."

"Not me," Peter countered.

"Not me either," Daphne chimed.

Abby laughed softly, although the laugh was bittersweet. "Nanny knows best. Come on. Up the stairs we go."

Just as she took each child by the hand, Stephen stepped back inside.

"Look, Daddy," Daphne said. "We're standing under the mistletoe. You have to kiss us."

Abby positioned each child under the plant and stepped back as he gave each a good night hug and kiss. Peter grabbed Abby's hand and gave her a tug forward.

"Now Abby has to kiss us," he said.

Her spirits brightening slightly, Abby kissed each child on the crown.

Then Peter tugged at his father's arm. "Now you have to kiss Daddy," he said.

Her cheeks warmed as she glanced nervously at Stephen. But instead of seeming embarrassed, his eyes were alight with mischief.

"I—I think your father has had enough kisses for one night," she stammered.

Ignoring her, Stephen stepped forward, cupped her cheeks in his hands, and kissed her playfully on the nose. Her heart somersaulted. The children giggled. For a moment, she stood frozen.

"It wasn't that bad, was it?" he asked with a devilish gleam in his eye.

"No, I—I don't think it was," she mumbled.

Her body still tingling, she quickly turned to the children. "Come," she said in her best nanny voice. "It's time for bed."

She quickly bathed Daphne, and as Peter splashed in the tub, she told the little girl a quick bedtime story. By the time she turned out the lights in Daphne's room, Peter was out of the tub and into his pajamas. He appeared in the hallway with his hair damp and ruffled.

"Come on," Abby said, "I'll tuck you in."

She stepped inside his room and plumped his pillow as he crawled between the sheets. Abby sat on the edge of his bed.

"Abby," he said, sitting up, "do you have to go back to England?"

An empty ache swelled in her chest. "Yes, Peter," she said, placing a hand on his cheek.

"But I don't want you to go," he said, his voice filled with tears. "Can't you just stay here with us?"

Abby swallowed hard. "Sometimes we can't always get what we want," she said gently. "We just have to get used to it. But I want you to know that I'll always love you."

"I love you," he said, throwing his arms around her neck.

She reveled in the sweetness of his child scent and the feel of his satiny cheek against hers. She swallowed the lump in her throat as she held him at arm's length. "You'll not only have Mrs. Bybee, but you'll have Aunt Kendall as well."

His chin crumpled. "Aunt Kendall doesn't like to finger paint. She's afraid she'll get paint on her clothes."

"What about Mrs. Bybee?"

"She's nice, like a grandma, but she doesn't like to walk in the rain."

Abby smiled ruefully. "Not many people do. In England, it rains as much as it does here. We love our walks so much that we can't let the weather keep us in."

"Why do people walk so much?" His eyes were wide with inquiry. "Don't they have cars?"

"Of course, but they walk for pleasure. There are lovely gardens to see and people to chat with. There are dogs to walk. Walking is good for you and makes you feel good. And you know what else?"

The boy shook his head.

"Walks can cheer you up when you feel sad."

The child lay back on his pillow. "I'm going to come see you, Abby, as soon as I can. Bobby Adams's father has a motorboat. He can take me."

She smiled. "I don't know of anyone I'd rather see." She tucked the quilt around his shoulders, then bent and kissed him on the forehead. "But I recommend that you take the Queen Elizabeth. The ride would be much smoother."

The boy smiled vaguely and closed his eyes.

"Good night, love," she whispered.

She rose quietly. She turned, then stiffened in surprise. Stephen stood in the doorway. He grinned sadly.

"I didn't really plan to eavesdrop," he said after they stepped out into the hall. He quietly closed Peter's door. "The boy's quite taken with you."

Abby felt another twinge of sadness, for Peter, for herself, for all of them, but quickly tried to cloak it. "He has good taste in women," she said.

Stephen grinned. "You sound like the Abby I first knew."

"I didn't think they would get attached in such a short time," she said. "But I suppose that's one of the occupational hazards of being a nanny. You know, Stephen, that I would never do anything to make them sad if I could help it."

"I know," he said, squeezing her arm. "I . . ." An awkward pause followed. "We'll all manage somehow." His hand dropped from her arm. "Good night, Abby."

"Good night," she said. She hurried to her room so he wouldn't detect the utter sense of loss she felt.

By the next afternoon, the twinkling tree lights and spicy scents of Christmas potpourri had failed to lift her spirits. Neither had helping Daphne compose a letter to Santa. All had the opposite effect. In less than three weeks, she would be out of the Krafts' lives forever.

It was just before four o'clock and Daphne was alternately putting her doll and the cat in a toy crib. After school, she'd walked Peter down the street to Bobby Adams's house. He was to be home at any moment.

But at ten after four, he hadn't yet arrived. She looked out the living room window, then stepped out the front door, but there was no sign of him. There was a clear view of the Adams house on the opposite side of the street. He'd probably just lost track of the time, she told herself.

She hurried back inside and rang Bobby's mother.

"Why, Abby," Marge Adams said. "He left a half hour ago. I watched as he crossed the street."

Abby's stomach clutched. "But he's not here. Did you see him come inside the house?"

"Why, no. I just watched until he stepped up on the sidewalk on the other side of the street."

"It's all right, Marge," she said. "I'm sure he's around somewhere. But it's not like Peter to be late."

Chilled, Abby hung up. She rushed upstairs and searched all the rooms. She checked downstairs, her heartbeat accelerating. She made a quick sweep of the backyard, but there was no sign of him.

"Daphne," she said, trying to keep her voice calm, "let's get your coat. We're going for a little walk."

"What about Peter?"

"Let's find him," Abby said.

With the little girl in tow, she checked the garage to no avail. Carrying Daphne, she rushed down the block calling him.

"But why won't he come, Abby?" Daphne asked, her voice bouncing along with Abby's hurried steps.

"Perhaps he can't hear us." She rushed a block in the opposite direction, but her cries were met only with silence.

Suddenly, Marge appeared from across the street. Her face was flushed with exertion, her short hair windblown.

"I've called some of the neighbors," she said, her eyes dim with concern. "No one's seen him. Abby, I'm so sorry. How could a little boy just vanish in just a few seconds?"

Abby, her body knotted with fear, shook her head.

"I can stay at your house with Daphne," Marge suggested, "so you can be free to look. I'll make some more calls."

Just as Abby consented, the Volvo rounded the corner. Her heart froze in her chest.

Stephen stepped out of the car, his eyes bright with anticipation. As she rushed to him, his expression crumpled. "Is something wrong?" he asked.

Abby's chest was tight and aching. "Stephen, Peter is missing."

Chapter Eleven

Stephen paled. "Missing?"

Abby was close to tears. "He was playing at Bobby Adams's and was supposed to have been home by four. Marge watched him cross the street, but after that, he seemed to disappear."

Stephen opened the car door and tossed his briefcase inside. "I'll make a sweep of the neighborhood. You call the police and call Kendall to watch Daphne so Marge can go home."

In a flash he was gone. Sick with worry, Abby ran to the telephone while Marge tried to reassure Daphne.

The police said they'd send a team of officers right away. Kendall, reached on her car phone, said she was on her way. The police arrived first.

"Let's make a list of his friends," said a kindly officer with salt-and-pepper hair. "Tell us his favorite places to go."

Abby clasped her hands to keep them from shaking.

"We've already called almost everywhere," she said, her voice unsteady.

But she answered their questions patiently. "He—he likes going for walks," she said, describing their route. "The school," she said, her heart leaping. "He loves to watch the construction crews as they do their digging." With equal force, her heart seemed to crash inside her chest. "It's so dangerous there."

The officer and his partner, a young woman, rose quickly. "Let's go check it out."

Kendall arrived just as they were leaving. Her pale blond hair was windblown, her cheeks flushed. Her icy look of disapproval made Abby's heart shrivel with guilt. "How could Peter have just disappeared?" she asked. "Isn't it your job to watch him?"

Abby's cheeks burned. "I do my best," she said weakly, her hands resting unsteadily on Daphne's shoulders.

Kendall took a sharp breath, then hung her tan cashmere coat on the hall tree with a snap. "Stephen must be frantic. He must be out looking."

"Yes," Abby said, her eyes burning with unshed tears. "Marge is going to go home and do what she can from there. If you'll stay with Daphne, I'll help with the search."

"I won't let her out of my sight," she said, giving Abby a piercing look. "What about the police?"

"They're on their way to the construction site."

Kendall's cool blue eyes narrowed. "Construction site?"

Abby explained Peter's interest in the excavation.

Kendall put her hand over her mouth. "Surely not."

A deep and raw guilt swept through Abby again as she struggled to hold back tears. It was she who had interested Peter in dinosaurs and archaeology. She threw on her raincoat and rushed outdoors. The rain, which had fallen heavily throughout the morning, had returned in large, intermittent drops.

She ran the six blocks to the site, looking for the boy everywhere along the way. She found the construction area flooded with searchlights from two police cars and a fire truck. She rushed through a split in the fence. She was stunned to see men quickly moving piles of wet earth with their bare hands. Her heart beating wildly, she ran toward the gaping hole in the ground. She heard a man yell just as she descended a ladder into the pit.

She landed ankle deep in the mud and before she knew it, she felt a tight grip on her arm pulling her up. "What are you doing here?" a man wearing a hard hat yelled, his face close to hers. His eyes flashed with anger. "You're going to get yourself hurt."

"I'm Peter's nanny. Tell me what you're doing!" she demanded. "Why are you digging?"

His expression became grim. "The rain caused some of the dirt to collapse. We're digging to see if anyone is under there."

Her knees turned to jelly. "But how . . ."

"The fence was cut—probably by vandals—and we found footprints leading into the pit. Some appeared to be small."

A wave of sickness washed over her and the evening turned even grayer.

"Come on, let's get you out of here," he said. "We're doing the best we can."

"No, I want to help," she insisted, wrenching away from him.

"Hey!" he called, running after her.

The mud made sucking noises as she struggled forward

into the glare of floodlights. She frantically joined the others, digging at the wall of earth that had collapsed from the side of the excavation. In her desperation, she was hardly aware that someone had placed a hard hat on her head and slipped the strap under her chin.

She dug until her arms ached. The rain soaked her hair and ran down her face, mixing with her tears. Her breath came in choking, exhausted gasps.

Then the floodlights flashed off and on.

"Stop!" a male voice cried through a megaphone. "The boy's been found. He's safe."

Abby went limp with relief. For a moment, she was so numb, she couldn't move until she felt a hand on her arm. Someone guided her up the ladder. Weak-kneed, she made it up to the top where a policeman reached for her hand.

"Where was he?" she asked weakly.

The officer patted her on the arm. "All I know is that someone found him not too far from here."

"And he's safe?" she asked, desperate for reassurance. "You're sure?"

"Yes," he said with a nod.

Suddenly, Stephen's voice rang through the air. "Abby!"

She looked up to find him running toward her. Wobbly with relief, she ran flying into his arms. "He's all right," she said breathlessly, reveling in the security of his embrace.

"I know," he said, holding her tightly. "Don't worry anymore."

She broke into tears of relief as he cradled her head against his shoulder. The rest of the world faded as he rocked her gently. At that moment, she wanted to never leave his arms.

But suddenly, in a flash of realization, she pulled away. She looked down to find herself covered with mud. Stephen's trenchcoat was soiled from holding her. "Oh, look what I've done," she said, half laughing and half crying.

"It's nothing," he said, pushing her wet hair back from her cheek. His gaze was piercing. "Let's go home."

Stephen drove over the dark, rain-slickened streets as quickly as conditions would allow. He explained how he had been driving and walking the streets and alleys of the neighborhood when Kendall had contacted him by car phone to tell him that police were searching the construction site. Just as he had arrived at the scene, he learned that Peter was safe.

"I didn't know you were in the pit until they helped you out," he said. "Abby, you could have been hurt."

"It didn't matter," she said. "All I wanted to do was find Peter."

He brought the car to a quick stop in the driveway and they scrambled out, not bothering to lock the doors. The front door of the house flew open and Peter bolted out, flinging himself in his father's arms. Abby's heart swelled.

Then the boy pulled away and ran to her. She held his small body close as she broke into tears. Stephen took him from her arms and carried him into the house as Abby followed.

"We were so worried, Peter," he said, his voice shaky. "Where were you?"

"In the Morgan twins' tree house." His hair was damp and his clothing soiled.

Kendall appeared in the entry with Daphne at her side. "Stephen, he was in there for an hour," she said, reaching up and giving him a quick kiss on the lips. "And he didn't have a jacket on." She gave Abby an indifferent glance.

Abby's cheeks flamed with guilt and shame. Trembling, she shed her muddy shoes and raincoat.

"Come on," Stephen said, still holding the boy. "Let's hear the whole story. What were you doing in Brent and Kent's tree house?"

Peter let his head fall against his father's shoulder. "It started to rain real hard. I rang the Morgans' doorbell, but no one was home, so I just climbed up in the tree house."

"Why didn't you come straight home like you were supposed to? This is not like you, Peter."

The boy frowned. "I wanted to be by myself," he said. "I went to where the new school is going to be, but the workers weren't there. I looked through the hole in the fence and then I started back home. Except when I got halfway home, it started to rain and that's when I got in the tree house. It was dark and wet and I was afraid to go out. Then the Morgans came home and they gave me a ride."

The stress lines on Stephen's face began to fade. "Peter, you must understand that you can't go off on long walks by yourself," he said firmly.

Peter heaved a little sigh. "Abby said that walks are good when you're feeling sad."

Abby's heart clutched. Kendall and Stephen briefly glanced at her. Stephen's look was benign, but Kendall's gaze was cooler than usual.

"You were feeling sad?" his father asked.

Peter nodded. "Abby is going away."

Abby's insides crumpled. "Peter, I'm so sorry," she said, but her words seemed inadequate.

"I did feel better until it started to rain," he said.

A faint smile touched Stephen's lips. "Will you promise you'll never try to take a walk by yourself again?"

The boy nodded, his head falling back against his father's shoulder.

"Let's get you cleaned up and into bed," Stephen said.

"I'll warm some milk for both of them," Abby said.

As she worked in the kitchen, she could hear Stephen and Kendall briefly speaking in tones too low to be audible. Then Kendall popped inside the kitchen door and bade Abby a perfunctory good-bye.

As Stephen bathed the children, guilt began to gnaw even more savagely at her insides. She'd committed a nanny's worst sin—losing sight of one of her charges. Although she'd taken measures to see that Peter got home from the Adamses' safely, she was still at fault.

She stirred a teaspoon of honey into each mug of hot milk and sprinkled cinnamon on top. She ached at the thought of letting Stephen down. She thought of his tight and lingering embrace at the construction site. But she knew that once his mind cleared, he would be angry with her. She thought of Kendall's cold stares and their whispers. And if professional humiliation weren't enough, her personal stature had been diminished as well. Hardly anything was more important than what Stephen and the children thought of her.

Stephen brought the children into the kitchen, rosy and subdued from their baths. His sleeves were rolled up; his face was etched with fatigue. Abby's eyes met his briefly, almost hesitantly. "There, children," she said, settling them in front of their mugs. "It's all nice and warm."

An uncharacteristic silence hung over the table as they drank. Abby prepared a mug of milk for Stephen, but she drank nothing. "Is everything better now?" she asked Peter, stroking his hair.

"A whole bunch," he said.

They quickly emptied their mugs. Abby kissed each of them good night before Stephen took them up to bed. Her heart ached as she tidied up the kitchen. He'd scarcely spoken to her.

She was getting ready to turn out the downstairs lights, when she heard his footsteps on the staircase. Her heartbeat quickened. How could she begin to apologize?

He appeared in the doorway, his pale eyes studying her seriously. "Abby—"

"Stephen," she interrupted, "I know there's no excuse for what happened. I can't tell you how terrible I feel. I'm so sorry for that hour's worth of misery I caused you. I wish more than anything that it had never happened."

"Abby, listen—"

"Stephen," she interrupted again, "please hear me out. If you like, I'll leave as soon as you can make other arrangements."

He took her firmly by the shoulders and shook her slightly. The dimple in his chin deepened as he looked at her sternly. "Abby, would you stop flogging yourself long enough to listen to me? I'm not going to fire you."

She blinked in surprise. "But you must be angry with me."

He sighed deeply. "I was. But when I saw you climbing out of that pit, I knew that Peter couldn't have meant much more to you than if he'd been your own child. How you managed to get beyond that police line is beyond me."

A lump rose to her throat. "If anything had happened . . ."

He gave her arm a gentle squeeze. "Don't think about it. He's safe. Now, let's both get some rest."

Placing an arm around her shoulder, he led her upstairs.

There was silence between then, but inside her chest, her heart screamed loudly.

The next day, she was sore and exhausted from the ordeal. There were shadows under Stephen's eyes and he was quieter than usual. He'd been kinder to her than she deserved, but she still feared he thought less of her.

After she ferried the children off to school, she went into the basement workshop and papered the walls of the dollhouse with scraps of wallpaper she'd gotten from Marge Adams. As she worked, she thought of how Stephen hadn't brought up Peter's reason for taking a walk. Of course, there was nothing to say. In two weeks, she would be gone. She would have to adjust and so would the children.

As she carefully measured the tiny walls, the telephone rang. Her legs ached as she ran up the basement stairs. She picked up the kitchen phone to hear Kendall's voice. Her stomach tightened.

"How are you, Abby?" Her tone was saccharine.

"Fine, thank you."

"I wonder if I might take the children one afternoon this week and buy them some Christmas outfits. In our family, we always celebrated Christmas like Easter—with new clothes. Besides, it will give me the opportunity to spend some time with them alone."

"If it's all right with Stephen, it's certainly all right with me."

"Yes, we discussed it just this morning," she said. "He suggested I check with you."

"Actually, this afternoon would be the most suitable," Abby responded. "Tomorrow, I take Boom to the vet and the children want to go along to give him some moral support, and on Friday, Stephen was to come home early and spend some time with them.''

''I suppose today will have to do, then,'' Kendall said. ''You'd be a dear if you could have them bundled up and ready to go by three-thirty.''

''They'll be ready,'' Abby promised.

She hung up, feeling a vague sense of unease. But she quickly chided herself. Hadn't she thought all along that Kendall should spend more time with the children?

Shortly before three-thirty, Kendall arrived wearing a long, sweeping red woolen coat with a small green Christmas wreath pin on the collar. The children had become slightly cross when they learned that they were going shopping instead of making Christmas cookies, but Abby promised them a surprise for the next day if they would be good.

''There, darlings,'' Kendall exclaimed, taking each by the hand. ''Let's go buy some beautiful things.''

As Abby had instructed, they left without protest.

For the next few hours, Abby was on edge. Would Kendall be holding their hands as they walked through the crowds? Would she watch their feet and fingers on elevators and escalators? Would she see that their caps were pulled down over their ears? Abby smiled ruefully at her own thoughts. She was as anxious as a new mother.

She finished papering the dollhouse by putting a few swatches of a miniature red-and-white print in the kitchen. As she stood back and admired her work, she heard footsteps upstairs. Fearing Daphne might discover the dollhouse, she quickly left the workshop, locked the door, and rushed upstairs. It was Stephen she found in the kitchen.

''Hello, Abby.'' His gaze flicked away from her. ''I hope I didn't frighten you.''

"You're home a little early," she said, conscious of her pounding pulse.

He shrugged. "Not by much."

"I must have lost track of the time," she said awkwardly. "I was working on the dollhouse."

His eyes showed a glint of interest, but there was something in the air between them that Abby couldn't define. Something had changed since yesterday. He was more reserved. She took it to mean that he'd lost faith in her, and she felt a stab of regret.

"Do you mind if I have a look?" he asked.

She shook her head and led the way down the basement. He was so close to her on the narrow staircase that she could almost feel his body heat. Her own temperature seemed to rise correspondingly. As she took the key from her pocket, Stephen took it from her hand. The brush of his fingers against hers made her heart jump.

He opened the door and switched on the light. "She'll love it," he said, standing back and examining the freshly papered rooms.

Abby wasn't looking at the dollhouse. She was looking at the solid set of shoulders in front of her. His familiar woodsy scent filled her with sadness. "I'll start on the curtains tomorrow," she said.

"Wonderful," he said with a smile. But his glance was fleeting, as if he didn't want to meet her eyes. "I appreciate this very much."

"It's the least I could do," she said, painfully reminded of what had happened the day before.

Just as they returned to the kitchen, Abby heard the front door open. Daphne's voice rang through the house. "Daddy! Abby!"

The little girl ran into her father's waiting arms and Peter put his arms around Abby's waist. She gave him a quick squeeze and glanced up to find Kendall emitting a deep sigh.

"Now I'm beginning to understand how my mother must have felt," Kendall said. Her hair, normally sleek, was slightly disheveled, her porcelainlike complexion flushed. "Children take more energy than I ever dreamed."

Stephen laughed. "Are you feeling your age at twenty-seven?"

"How do people manage without help?"

"Most do," Stephen said. "Now, let's see what you bought."

Kendall opened a box and lifted a little black velvet dress with a white lace collar from folds of tissue paper. A second box contained dark gray pants for Peter, and a red blazer with a crest. "Aren't they darling?" she asked.

"Quite nice," Abby acknowledged.

Kendall gazed dreamily at Stephen. "I thought perhaps a Christmas portrait would be in order—for the four of us."

Stephen pulled Daphne closer, but said nothing.

Suddenly feeling as if she didn't belong in the room, Abby swallowed hard. "You children must be hungry," she said.

Peter shook his head. "Aunt Kendall bought us some chocolates—from Bellevue."

Kendall smiled. "Belgium, sweet."

Abby felt a twinge of annoyance. "Well, come, then," she said, reaching for the children's hands. "Let's go for a walk and see if we can work up some appetites."

They walked briskly as the children told her of all the toys they'd seen. When they returned about twenty minutes later, Stephen and Kendall were standing by her little red sports car. As Abby walked up the driveway with the children, she couldn't help but overhear Kendall. Other than the words "wedding" and "getting things in order," she could comprehend little.

Her heart contracted. It was inevitable that Stephen and Kendall would marry. If only she could put it out of her mind and concentrate on her own future. But it was always there, like a dull, incessant ache.

She'd just began preparing the children a light supper of scrambled eggs and toast when Stephen came into the kitchen. She'd heard him speaking to the children in the living room as they played on the floor. His jaw was firm, his hands thrust deeply into his pockets.

"I hope you don't mind something light," she said, trying to sound cheerful. "I have some very nice shaved ham as well."

His expression was one of distraction. "Anything is fine," he said, sitting down. He crossed one long leg over another.

"Some hot tea perhaps?" she asked, reaching into the refrigerator.

There was a brief pause. "Abby," he said, ignoring her earlier question, "do you have plans for the weekend?"

She set the package of ham on the counter and turned toward him. "Nothing special."

"I'm taking the children to the cabin for a little skiing. The Carringtons are going to Hawaii and there will be no one there except for Mr. Grinstead, the caretaker, who will be in and out. Would you please be our guest?"

"But I wouldn't want to be in the way," she protested.

"You wouldn't. And take heed of the fact that I'm asking you to go as a guest and not as a nanny. *I'll* be the nanny, and as for food, the freezer will be stocked with Nadine Carrington's treats."

"But this time should be just for you, Kendall, and the children," she insisted.

His lips tightened. "Kendall won't be there. She has a group of friends that she goes to Colorado with every year at this time and, well," he added with a shrug, "traditions are traditions."

Emotions were battering her. It was time to wean herself away from this family. A weekend with them in a mountain cabin, knowing that in two weeks she would be gone, would be difficult. Yet she wanted to cling to every minute despite the emotional cost. She hesitated for a moment. "I would be pleased to be your guest," she said.

His pale eyes brightened. "That's what I wanted to hear."

The cabin wasn't a cabin at all but a log house with floor-to-ceiling windows framed in green, balconies on three levels, and a terrace. It sat amid towering pines and banks of fresh, sugarlike snow. A garland of cedar, caught with bows at each corner, hung over the front door.

"Nadine doesn't miss a detail," Stephen remarked as they eased up the steep drive in a rented four-wheel-drive vehicle. The car was loaded with rented ski equipment, including a hot-pink ski outfit for Abby. Both children were strapped in the backseat.

"How lovely," Abby marveled. "The house seems to belong here."

"That was my plan when I designed it," he said, parking. "I'm glad you like it."

Abby got out of the car and was immediately invigorated by the sharp, clear air. Stephen, wearing snug, faded jeans, hiking boots, and a heavy red plaid flannel shirt rolled up at the elbows, lifted the children out of the car. Even through the thermal undershirt he wore, Abby could see the strong muscles of his forearms at play, and her insides stirred. Then a sinking realization hit her. These were the memories she would have to be content with.

"Let's ski, Daddy!" Peter squealed.

"As soon as we unload, son."

Stephen, carrying a backpack and other gear, ascended the steps as Abby and the children followed. He unlocked the door and Abby stepped inside. She stopped, absently letting her tote bag drop to the floor. The log walls were left unfinished and natural light bathed the room. The furniture was an eclectic mixture of wicker and overstuffed pieces. Indian rugs hung from the walls, from the railing enclosing the loft, and were scattered over the pine floor. The centerpiece of the room was a large stone fireplace.

"Do you like it?" Stephen asked.

"Oh, yes," she marveled, too astounded to say much else.

He laughed softly. "We can enjoy it later. Let's get into our ski clothes. The children are anxious to start."

He showed her to a small bedroom on the second level where she opened the box of rented ski clothing he'd brought for her after getting a list of her sizes. She dressed with uncertainty, not quite sure what to do with what. There were ski socks and liners, thermal underwear, a one-piece ski suit, a matching hot-pink headband which she snapped around her dark hair, mittens, a neck gaiter, and sunscreen. Then there were the boots. They fit. She just couldn't walk in them.

She made her way gingerly down the hall. In an adjoining bedroom, Stephen was outfitting the children. Peter was dressed in bright blue. Daphne was being zipped into a pink suit similar to Abby's. Stephen, still in his jeans, turned to find Abby standing over him. He rose slowly, eyeing her frankly from head to toe.

"Is something on backwards?" Abby asked.

He smiled sheepishly. "No, everything is in perfect order."

Her cheeks tingling slightly, she took the children downstairs. A few minutes later, Stephen emerged wearing a black ski suit and white turtleneck. A quick glance showed his hair was appealingly tousled, then she turned away to avoid appearing interested.

Outside, she watched as he helped Peter with his skis and Daphne with her toboggan. The gently rolling landscape near the cabin provided what appeared to Abby to be a safe place for them. Stephen reminded the children of the basics and to Abby's amazement, they took off fearlessly.

"Now it's your turn," he said, turning toward her. The sunlight brought out the golden highlights of his hair.

"I don't know the first thing," she protested.

"I'll show you," he said, helping her attach her boots to the skis.

She mimicked his movements as they shuffled uphill, using the poles for support.

"Now," he said gently, "remember that the people in front of you have the right of way. It's your job to avoid them, not the other way around. If you have to stop, do it by sitting or falling. That will do until you get better at this."

At the foot of the hill, she could see the children happily trekking back up.

"Let's work on your wedge," he said, moving close to her.

His nearness made her blood rush. "Wedge?"

"Place your skis so they'll look like a V with the tips together and the tails apart." He took her firmly by the shoulders as she awkwardly shifted around. "You have to force your knees to exert pressure on the skis' inside edges."

Abby looked at him with trepidation, but before she could back out, he gave her a gentle shove and she went sailing down the incline with a speed that accelerated quickly. In her excitement, her weight shifted and she lost her balance. Her heart seemed to leap out of her chest as she went down in a blur, skis clattering and snow flying. She hit the ground with a hard thump and rolled, her face stinging with snow. In an instant, she heard the whoosh of skis and Stephen yelling her name. He fell to her side, rolling into her. He turned over and propped himself up, his face over hers.

"Are you all right?" he asked, his eyes narrow with concern. His face was within inches of hers.

"I think so," she said, smiling weakly. "Nothing feels broken."

He took off his mittens and brushed the snow from her cheek and her hair. Their eyes caught and the snow seemed to melt underneath her. Stephen's fingers lingered on her cheek and his thumb swept over her lower lip. Her blood went wild in her veins. As he slowly lowered his mouth toward hers, each beat of her heart grew louder in anticipation.

"Daddy!" Daphne's voice rang through the air.

Stephen jerked away. Abby, her heart in her throat, sat up to see the little girl running toward them. "I saw a bunny!"

Stephen stood up, his face flushed. Avoiding her eyes,

he helped Abby to her feet. "That's exciting," he said. "Maybe he'll come back."

Daphne stepped closer and looked at Abby curiously. "Did Abby fall down and hurt herself?"

"I'm fine, sweetheart," Abby said shakily.

"I want to play some more," Daphne said, absently cavorting off.

At that moment, Peter appeared, needing an adjustment on his skis. Stephen turned away, leaving things even more awkward between Abby and him.

For the next half hour, they diverted their attention to the children, clumsily avoiding each other. Abby made a few more runs on her skis, this time without falling, but her heart still hammered with the memory of his lips so close to hers. She avoided his eyes. She avoided even looking in his direction except when he zoomed skillfully down the little slope.

"Let's go in and warm up," he said finally. "Nadine said there would be cider and cocoa in the refrigerator."

"Let me get it, please," she said. She removed her skis and went inside the cabin.

Her hands trembled as she took the mugs out of the cabinets. He had been going to kiss her. There was no question about it. Her cheeks stung as she replayed the scene in her mind. What did he think she was? He was all but engaged to Kendall. She felt the raw burn of indignation, but underneath it the unmistakable flame of longing.

She stayed in the cabin the rest of the afternoon while Stephen played outside with the children. He had started a fire in the fireplace and she sat curled on the sofa with a new mystery novel. But she couldn't concentrate. She could only think of the way his eyes had fixed magnetically on hers.

They had an early supper. Nadine had left lasagna in the refrigerator and Stephen had insisted on preparing the rest. He occupied himself in the kitchen while Abby watched the children. Since they were tired from a day in the snow, he put them to bed early, but not without their insisting that Abby come up and kiss them good night.

"Perhaps I should turn in too," she said as he closed the door to the children's room. "Good night, Stephen." She quickly turning away. But he caught her by the arm and pulled her closer.

"We need to have a talk." His eyes were intense. "Please come downstairs."

Without protest, she led the way and sat in a large wicker chair by the fire. But he took her hand and pulled her to her feet. The room was dark except for the golden glow from the burning logs. "Abby, about this afternoon . . ."

Her cheeks heated. "You want to apologize. It was a momentary lapse. You weren't thinking."

He pulled her close. "No, I don't want to apologize."

Stunned, she stared at him.

"I'm not sorry I tried to kiss you," he said, his eyes bright with intensity. "I'm only sorry I didn't succeed."

Before she could say a word, he gently tilted her chin and touched his mouth to hers with the delicate sweetness of a flower.

Chapter Twelve

The kiss was short and tentative, but it was quickly followed by another that took such possession of her that the rest of the world seemed to vanish. His lips played on hers with such longing that she was stunned. *Can this really be happening?* she asked herself. The kiss, warm and sensual, seemed to come from the foggy recesses of a dream.

Turbulent emotions swept over her in stormy waves. All rational thought stopped, overtaken by the thundering language of the heart.

She slipped her arms around him and felt the heat pulsing in the strong muscles of his back. She surrendered to his touch, letting him envelop her in his arms. His embrace was so tender, yet sure, that she lost herself in it.

Suddenly, reality forced its way back into her consciousness and her mind snapped with realization. She was not only kissing her employer but a man who talked of marrying another woman. She went cold with alarm. Trembling, she pushed herself away from him. She stared at him for a long, smoldering moment.

His eyes, dusky with desire, probed her face. His brow crinkled in confusion. "Abby, what's wrong?"

Her chest heaved. "Everything."

He sighed, then turned away from her, absently pacing back and forth. He ran a hand over his jaw, then glanced at her again, his expression somber. "Forgive me. I had no right to do that."

Abby's heart continued to beat a tattoo in her chest. "No, you didn't," she said, feeling a swell of anger. "You were firm about not wanting nannies to take an interest in you. I've done my best to abide by that rule and now look what you've done . . ." She threw out her hands in exasperation. "Do you kiss all the nannies?"

His jaw hardened. "There have only been two, counting Mrs. Bybee, and the answer is no. You're the only one I've ever kissed and I'm deeply sorry for having offended you. It was inexcusable. I wouldn't blame you if you never forgave me."

"To make matters worse, there's Kendall," she said tonelessly.

He began to pace again, massaging his forehead with his fingertips as if he were in pain. Even through her anger, Abby's blood raced at the mere sight of him—his long legs, his solid shoulders, and the finely chiseled profile. Then he stopped and gazed at her, his eyes filled with conviction. "Don't think that I don't care about you, Abby. Don't think that I was just indulging a whim. I don't make it a practice of kissing women just because the opportunity is there."

"Then why did you do it?" she asked. There were tears in her voice.

He looked at her darkly and swallowed hard. "Because lately I've come to realize how much I'm going to miss you. In my life, I've had to say good-bye to too many people before I was ready. I'd lost both of my parents by the time I was twenty-seven. Then I lost Diane. I'm not very good at giving people up.''

Her throat felt raw. She struggled to keep her emotions from prevailing over logic. ''You are fortunate that you will have Mrs. Bybee once again. And after the wedding, you and the children will have Kendall.''

He gazed at her in silence for a moment. ''Perhaps we should go to bed,'' he said. ''We'll both be more clear-headed in the morning.''

''Good night, Stephen,'' she said stiffly.

He reached out as if to touch her cheek, then pulled his hand back. ''Good night, Abby.''

The kiss burned on her lips long after she'd gone to bed. Ever mindful of the fact that Stephen lay just feet away in the next room, she couldn't sleep. In the shadows of the night, the realization came to her with the chilling force of an Arctic wind. She was in love.

Her chest heaved with pent-up emotion. At first, she'd been sure that her heart was impervious to such a man. This buttoned-down, nose-to-the-grindstone architect seemed to have no interests outside his work and his children. He didn't laugh easily. He didn't suffer Abby's cheekiness gladly. Then something began to happen and the man of steel began to turn into flesh and blood. When that happened, Abby found herself losing control of her heart.

She stared at the ceiling in sick realization. In two weeks, she'd probably never see him again. It was the losses of the past that led him to kiss her, not the emotions of the present. It was simply a parting gesture, nothing more. She loved him and his children and she would have to live the rest of her life content with being part of their lives for a mere three months.

She choked back her sobs, vowing to take it the proper English way—with a stiff upper lip. But the tears sneaked down her cheeks until finally, in exhaustion, she succumbed to sleep.

She awoke the next morning longing for the comforting embrace of Aunt Margo. It was then that the idea flashed in her mind. She would go to Texas for Christmas instead of waiting until her last week in America. It would take her out of the Kraft house at a time when her emotions were raw and when the spirit of Christmas would clash painfully with her own flagging spirits. Besides, it was a time for Stephen and Kendall to be together. It was a time for families.

It wasn't quite dawn when she got up. She threw on jeans and her fisherman's sweater and padded softly down the hallway in heavy woolen socks. The cabin was eerily quiet. Outside, not even a squirrel chattered.

As she descended the stairs, her heart beat rapidly with thoughts of the night before. Her mind spun. How could she make sense out of a kiss like that? In terms of her own reaction, there was no mystery. She responded because she was helpless not to, because she loved him.

When she got to the bottom step, she froze. Sitting alone in the dark in front of a flickering fireplace was Stephen. Just as she turned to sneak back to her room, he called her name.

Her spine stiffened. "I didn't mean to disturb you," she said, her voice faltering. She walked cautiously toward him.

"I thought I'd watch the sun rise," he said. "I designed the cabin with this in mind. It's not often I can spend the night in one of my own buildings and actually experience how well the design works.''

Abby glanced at the large window facing east where the mountain was beginning to show a rim of gold. ''The view is lovely,'' she said.

''Come sit down,'' he said.

''I really should be . . .''

''You shouldn't be doing anything,'' he said. ''You're the guest. I'm the host. In a few moments, we'll have coffee. Sit down, please.''

She sat in a chair next to his, turning it slightly to face the sunrise. In the slowly expanding light, she could see that his hair was rumpled, his face still unshaven. His look of boyish vulnerability sent a dull ache through her. Suddenly, she could think of nothing to say.

Stephen broke the silence. ''Times like this make me wish I could paint. Look at how the light seems to change from minute to minute, becoming more vibrant, taking on more tones of color. The sun looks like a gold coin tucked behind the mountain.'' His eyes stayed fixed on the scene outdoors.

''You sound more like a poet than an artist,'' she said.

He glanced at her with just a hint of a smile in his eyes. Her heart skittered. ''The girls in school did like my valentines.''

Her stomach tightened with the reminder that this was a man who could have almost any woman he wanted. He might have kissed her, but it was Kendall who would be his wife.

She took a deep breath to compose herself. ''Stephen, I'd like to talk to you about Christmas,'' she began.

His eyes stayed focused on the window. ''Don't worry

about anything, Abby. It's being catered. Kendall is engineering the whole event.''

"That's not what I mean," she responded. "I'd like a week off to spend Christmas with my Aunt Margo.''

He quickly turned from the window and studied her with narrowed eyes. ''The children will be disappointed that you won't be with them for Christmas.''

She experienced a sinking feeling. Would only the children miss her? ''I don't mean to disappoint them, but perhaps it's better if I separate myself from them gradually. They can get used to my being gone, then I can come back again to say good-bye. After Christmas, I'll have one more week with them before Mrs. Bybee comes back.''

The golden glow of the sunrise began to fill the room, but Stephen didn't seem to notice. As the room brightened, Abby was able to see that there were circles under his eyes and that his face was etched with fatigue. ''Surely I must be a factor in your change of plans. You must not know what to think of me.''

For a moment she was at a loss for words. ''Aunt Margo doesn't have any family to share Christmas with,'' she said obliquely. She didn't tell him that Aunt Margo didn't yet know she would be there for Christmas. She also knew her plans didn't make sense from a logistical standpoint, that the shortest route to London wasn't to Dallas, then back to Seattle again. But nothing in her life was making much sense now. All she knew was that if she spent Christmas with the Krafts, her heart might break in full view of everyone.

He ran a hand over a stubbled cheek. ''I want you to do whatever makes you happy. I'll take care of the children.''

She swallowed hard. ''Thank you, Stephen.''

A brief, yet awkward, silence followed. She glanced at

his troubled face and an ache tightened across her chest. She rose to check on the children.

"Abby," he said finally, "as for me, you're not obligated to explain anything. Whatever you're feeling about me, however bad, is justified. I apologize once again."

She responded with a pained gaze. "I appreciate the gesture. If you'll excuse me, I'll look in on the children."

They spent much of Sunday outdoors. Abby watched as Stephen patiently helped Daphne learn to ski. He seemed not to notice Abby as she sat on the deck of the cabin breathing in the crisp mountain air. Her book was open in her lap, but she was ever-conscious of Stephen silhouetted against the sparkling snow. Peter, on skis, had left a web of tracks all over the little incline.

They drove home chattering to the children but saying little to each other. What irony, Abby thought, that a kiss could drive two people apart.

Abby glanced furtively at him. His jaw was firmly set, his eyes carefully trained on the road. At times, she could sense that he was glancing at her, but she dared not look into his eyes.

"I'll talk to Mrs. Bybee this week to make sure everything is in order," he said finally. "We talked two weeks ago. Her daughter is recovering nicely and Mrs. Bybee expects to be able to come back on schedule."

A gray cloud seemed to materialize around her. Suddenly it made Abby's leaving seem more like a business than anything else. He'd been right about cautioning her about becoming emotionally involved. This was a business relationship and nothing else.

Within an hour, they were home again. The front lawn was dusted with snow and the house, with a fresh bayberry wreath on the door, looked especially welcoming. But Abby reminded herself with a twinge of pain that it wouldn't be long before she would soon walk out the front door for good.

As she settled the children down with some hot chocolate and Stephen put their gear away, the doorbell rang. Abby found Kendall standing on the porch in her flowing red coat. She smiled perfunctorily, her lips flawlessly tinted and glossed. "Hello, Abby."

She greeted Kendall politely. "Please come in. Stephen should be down at any moment."

"Here he is now," Kendall said, glancing over Abby's shoulder.

Abby turned to see Stephen rapidly descending the stairs.

"Hello, darling," Kendall called. Abby couldn't help but notice a tightness in her voice.

"Hello, Kendall," he said, stopping on the bottom step. "How did it go with your friends in Colorado?"

Abby turned to leave, but at that moment, Abby noticed that Daphne's ski cap lay on the floor. She bent over to pick it up.

"Aren't you going to kiss me?" Abby overheard Kendall ask.

As she tucked the cap in Daphne's coat sleeve, she caught a glimpse of Stephen touching his lips to Kendall's. Her heart ached with a deep rawness and she quickly left the room. The twinkling lights of the Christmas tree seemed to mock her.

Abby stayed in the kitchen with the children while Kendall and Stephen talked in the entry. Abby couldn't help think it odd that Kendall hadn't come in to say hello to them.

"Abby," Daphne asked quizzically, "can we stay up all

night to catch Santa Claus coming down the chimney?'' She wore a cocoa mustache.

"You'll have to ask your father," she said. "You know, I've heard that Santa won't visit children who aren't tucked in their beds."

Daphne's eyes widened. "Then maybe you can stay up and take a picture of him."

Abby swallowed hard. "Children, I know you're going to be disappointed, but I won't be here for Christmas. You see, my Aunt Margo has no family and she's on a big Texas ranch all alone except for the ranch hands. I'm going to be with her. I'm very sorry, but I hope you understand."

Their faces clouded with disappointment. "But she can come here," Peter said, his eyes alight with the idea.

She smiled ruefully. "It's really best that I go there. You'll have a splendid Christmas with your father and your Aunt Kendall. Then I'll come back again to say good-bye."

Daphne frowned. "Don't go, Abby. We love you."

A lump rose in her throat. "And I love you and I'll miss you more than you know. But I must go. England is my home."

"You'll open your presents before you go, won't you?" Peter asked. "We got you three. It's supposed to be a secret."

Before she could answer, Kendall popped her head into the kitchen. "How are my little ones? Did you have a nice time at the cabin?"

Peter nodded, somewhat listlessly. Daphne poked a finger into her cocoa.

"That's wonderful," Kendall said, seemingly oblivious to their mood. Abby noticed that her skin was lightly tanned. "Colorado was so much fun. It was so nice to see my friends again."

Stephen appeared in the doorway, glancing first at the children, then Abby. Their eyes caught for a brief but jarring moment.

"Would you two like some cocoa?" Abby asked, struggling to regain her senses.

"Thank you, Abby, but I have to run," Kendall said. She walked around the table and kissed each child on the crown. "Aunt Kendall loves you," she said.

She gave Stephen a quick kiss and was gone.

Abby's news that she would be in Texas in time for Christmas was greeted with a Texas-size whoop from Aunt Margo. In just two days, she'd be on her way.

In the meantime, she took walks with the children, savoring every moment. One day, she took them to buy gifts for Boom. They chose a toy mouse and a purple collar with a bell.

Since the trip to the cabin, Stephen had become quieter and more focused on Peter and Daphne. Abby, too, found herself using the children as a shield. If she kept busy with them, she could avoid being alone with their father. Their conversation was polite, yet awkward, and though they spoke of everyday matters, Abby knew that they were both thinking of what had happened between them.

She was alone with the children for two evenings while Stephen and Kendall went out. But on the day before she was to leave for Texas, Stephen said the children wanted to celebrate an early Christmas with her.

That evening, Stephen insisted that she wait downstairs while they made the preparations. She sat on the edge of the sofa watching Boom bat an ornament with his paw. The tiny white lights on the Christmas tree twinkled like a thousand stars. In the background were the strains of "Rudolph the Red-Nosed Reindeer.'' Almost every decoration bore Kendall's imprint. Abby had the odd sensation of being on the outside of Christmas looking in.

She heard footsteps on the stairs, then turned to find Daphne and Peter dressed in their Christmas outfits and walking toward her. Each carried a gift and smiled brightly. Behind them was Stephen, his eyes shining mysteriously.

"Merry Christmas, Abby," they said in unison, holding out the gifts.

Her heart jumped. "You children shouldn't have . . . ," she said.

"Open them," Daphne said merrily, her white, lacy collar bouncing as she jumped up and down.

Peter, wearing his red blazer and tugging uncomfortably at the collar of his shirt, nodded eagerly. She looked at Stephen, and his wan smile tore at her heart.

"I can hardly wait," she said, injecting cheer into her voice.

She sat in a chair next to the tree while they gathered around her. To the strains of "Frosty the Snowman," Abby opened Daphne's first. A small card read, *Merry Christmas. I love you.* A lump rose in her throat as she gave the child a quick kiss.

"Hurry, Abby," Daphne said, twisting about in a new pair of Mary Janes.

She tore open the package to find a picture book of English country cottages. She fanned through the pages. "Oh, Daphne," she said, "it's so lovely. It's just like home."

The little girl's eyes shone. "Daddy helped me."

Abby glanced at Stephen, her heart leaping painfully at the sight of his pale eyes. "It's perfect," she said.

"Open mine, Abby," Peter interjected.

Shaky with emotion, she quickly untied the red ribbon

on the gold box to find a stuffed toy dinosaur. A lump rose in her throat. "Both of you couldn't have gotten anything to please me more."

She held them close as the tears burned at her eyes.

Stephen handed her a third gift. "It's a little something from me."

Her heart scampered to her throat. She didn't trust her voice to speak. With trembling fingers, she opened it to find an antique music box that played a lilting tune.

"It's vintage," he said.

"It's beautiful. Thank you so much." She dared not look at Stephen although she could feel his eyes on her. She knew that just one look would start a torrent of tears.

Tumbleweed Ranch was a four-thousand-acre spread on the central Texas plains. There was little but earth and sky except for occasional stands of trees that stood barren, spiky and determined against the wind. Aunt Margo's house, a rambling, turn-of-the-century two-story with a porch swing, stood not far past a black iron arch bearing the ranch's name. Ralphie, her border collie, came leaping off the porch.

Abby got out of her aunt's old Suburban, greeted the dog, and went to the back hatch to get her luggage.

Aunt Margo took her by the shoulders. "Let me get a good look at you," she said, her crimson lips pursed. "Just as pretty as ever, but you need a little fattening up."

"Oh, Aunt Margo," she protested, "I'm not a beef cow."

"You look strained, dear. Is something bothering you? Are those two kids a handful?"

Abby shook her head. "They're wonderful children."

"What about their father?"

An ache spread across her chest. "He's very good with them," she said obliquely.

Aunt Margo studied her face as if she were a child who might not be telling the whole truth. "Maybe you just need a little Texas sunshine," she said, picking up Abby's suitcase. "Let's get you settled in and rested up."

There was no hint of Christmas on the front door, where no wreath hung, nor on the porch, where there were no lights. But when Aunt Margo threw open the door, Abby gasped. The stairway was decorated with red bows and a garland and the entry smelled of cinnamon and evergreen. In the old-fashioned parlor to the right, a garland swagged from the crown molding. Every few feet, it was caught by red-and-green plaid bows. A large tree stood in one corner, the star on top grazing the high ceiling. It was covered with so many ornaments that the cedar branches were almost hidden.

Around the room were angels of all sorts—stuffed, ceramic, and plastic. Some were painted on plates, some on cards and tinware.

"Welcome back to the Tumbleweed," Aunt Margo said with a hug. "I'm delighted you're here."

They spent the afternoon chatting about family memories and looking at photo albums while drinking wassail and nibbling homemade cookies.

Despite the comfort she found in being with Aunt Margo, thoughts of Stephen brought frequent surges of pain.

The next afternoon, Aunt Margo held a party for the four ranch hands: Slim, the foreman, a wiry man in his sixties; Hal and Hank, forty-year-old bachelor twins; and Kip, a broad-shouldered, leggy cowboy close to Abby's age.

Kip's eyes flashed with interest. "Can you slide down a banister like Mary Poppins?"

"I don't do banisters, I'm afraid."

"You do a nice English accent."

Abby looked at him with mild amusement. "I've had a lifetime of practice."

After the party was over and Aunt Margo had given each a generous Christmas bonus, Abby helped her clean up.

"I think Kip was taken with you," the older woman said. "In fact, he asked me if he might take you to a movie."

Abby turned to her aunt in mild alarm. "It's very kind of him but I would rather stay here."

"You'd rather be with me than with a handsome cowboy? I'm flattered, dear, but you're going to disappoint a nice young man."

"I'm really sorry, but my heart just isn't in it."

Aunt Margo responded with uncharacteristic silence.

On Christmas Eve, Abby gave Aunt Margo a silk scarf and an imported plum pudding. Margo gave Abby a restored portrait of herself and Abby's father as children. She also gave her a Fifties-era cowboy shirt to add to her vintage clothing collection. Christmas carols played softly on the radio. The older woman talked of life on the ranch while Ralphie snoozed disinterestedly nearby.

Aunt Margo reached over and switched off the lamp, so that the only light came from the Christmas tree. "Your father always enjoyed looking at the tree in the dark."

Abby's heart ached as she studied the tree's colorful radiance. It not only ached for her father, but for another man she loved. She imagined his children in their beds, hardly able to sleep for the excitement. How she yearned to kiss their satiny cheeks.

"Abby," Aunt Margo began, "won't you tell me what's

wrong? This is the first Christmas without your father, I know, but I sense it goes deeper than that.''

There was a moment of silence. Then Abby took a deep breath. ''I'm afraid I've grown too attached to the Kraft family.''

Aunt Margo turned the light back on. ''But in one of your letters, you told me you didn't get along very well with the father.''

Her cheeks tingled. ''I didn't.''

''And now you're going to miss him?''

Abby frowned. ''It's so hard to explain.''

The older woman rose from her chair and sat next to Abby on the sofa. She put her arm around her. ''Maybe I can help you. You've grown attached not only to the children, but to the father as well.''

Abby nodded painfully.

''Dear, do tell me what do you mean by 'attached.' ''

Her chest tightened. ''Very attached. As attached as one can get.''

Aunt Margo bit her bottom lip. ''In Texas, we call that being in love. Isn't that what they say in England, too?''

A tear slid down Abby's cheek. ''Oh, Aunt Margo! What am I going to do?''

The older woman put her arms around her and kissed her forehead. ''If it's meant to be, it will be.''

Abby shook her head adamantly. ''It's hopeless,'' she said, her cheeks now wet with tears.

Fighting to maintain her composure, she told of Stephen's relationship with Kendall.

''I'm so sorry, dear,'' Aunt Margo said. ''But you *will* get through this somehow. We're all stronger than we think. That's something I learned when your Uncle Ed died. I survived and you will, too.''

* * *

Abby survived Christmas Day without a tear. They delivered baked goods to a nursing home and Aunt Margo and a group of friends sang carols to the oldsters.

Peter and Daphne had no doubt opened the gifts she'd left in addition to the books she'd given them the night before she left Seattle. She hoped Stephen liked the fountain pen she'd given him. She'd brought the music box to Texas, but couldn't bear to take it out of her suitcase.

The end of Christmas brought a mild sense of relief. The next day, while Aunt Margo tended to the ranch payroll, Abby set off for a walk with Ralphie.

"The fresh air and exercise will do you some good," the older woman said. "Take your time. Take the trail up to the big pond. There are lots of birds. I've put out feeders."

Abby, outfitted in hiking boots, woolen leggings, a turtleneck, and a red plaid wool shirt that had belonged to Uncle Ed, set off with the collie trotting happily ahead. In the distance, she could see Slim mending a fence, and gave him a friendly wave.

The sky was overcast, but the weather was mild. The prairie reached as far as the eye could see. She quickened her gait as if to distance herself more from her problems. Within twenty minutes she reached the pond, where as a child, she'd been fascinated by the tadpoles wriggling at the water's edge.

Abby sat on the bank. Birds twittered in a nearby stand of trees. Ralphie chased after them as she let the balmy Texas breeze play through her hair. Time slipped away as she watched the clouds and thought of Stephen.

She felt utterly raw inside. How could he have kissed her if he loved someone else? Her cheeks burned. What kind of a man was he? What kind of a woman was she to melt into his arms? She felt a creeping sense of shame. This was not a man who kissed casually and for amusement. Yet his kissing her made no sense at all.

"Abby?" His voice seemed to ride on the wind and follow her everywhere. His rich tones seemed to come from a dream.

"Abby . . ."

Ralphie barked and she turned. Coming toward her was a tall and familiar form, a man with glints of gold in his hair. She stood, blinking in disbelief. It was not until she heard his footsteps that she realized the man was real.

She walked toward him, her heart beating like a thousand drums. "Stephen, is that you?"

"Yes, Abby," he said, his steps quickening.

She ran to meet him, stopping just short of his open arms. His eyes darkened. "The children . . ." she said. "Are they all right?"

He placed his hands on her shoulders. "They couldn't be better."

She searched his face, still not quite believing he was there. His eyes were bright and full of longing. Her heart fluttered. "Why have you come? Is there a problem with Mrs. Bybee?" She tried to pull away but his hold on her was firm. She turned her head to avoid his eyes.

He placed a hand on her chin and forced her to look at him. His brows were furrowed, his chin crinkled. "Abby, I'm here for only one reason—you."

She searched his eyes for meaning. "I don't understand."

"Didn't you understand when I kissed you that night?"

"No," she said, an ache spreading across her chest. "You needn't have come all this way to apologize again."

He pulled her closer. "I kissed you because I love you."

She was stunned into silence. "But there's Kendall . . ." she said finally.

He shook his head. "Kendall and I finally admitted the truth. We're not right for each other. We sensed it all along, but our sense of obligation to Diane's wishes led to our deceiving ourselves and each other.

"You see, Abby, after Diane died, I was so grief-stricken that I wanted to see Diane in Kendall. They were nothing alike but Kendall was always there when I needed her. The relationship was comfortable. Love wasn't my objective, because I didn't think I could ever love anyone but Diane. The objective was to uphold Diane's wish that her family be involved with raising the children.

"Then there was the terrible guilt that I felt. Diane didn't want to go on that trip with her parents, but I insisted. For a long time, I blamed myself for her death, and not to go along with her wishes about raising the children seemed unthinkable.

"Now, as it turns out, Kendall has admitted she would rather be an aunt than a mother. Her freedom and her social life are more important than she realized. It was a difficult decision for her.

"At the same time, I was acknowledging some truths of my own. You were the one I was coming home to every day. You were zipping about in those crazy outfits and thoroughly enjoying the children. The fact that you didn't seem to care if I existed attracted me to you in an odd sort of way. As it turns out, you brought me back to life again, Abby. You made me laugh again. You made me love again."

Her heart leaped for joy. "Oh, Stephen," she said, melting into his arms. "I love you. I tried so hard not to."

He grinned crookedly. "I'm delighted you failed," he said, cradling her face in his hands. His mouth settled on hers with a hunger and yearning that almost took her breath away. Her heart pounded in her ears.

He pulled away, his breath ragged. "Your love for the children made me see you as a woman, not as a nanny. I love you, Abby. You'll marry me, won't you?"

Her heart took flight like a bird. A rush of joy almost lifted her off her feet. Then a cloud of doubt swiftly eclipsed her happiness. Her body stiffened in his arms.

"What's wrong, sweetheart?" he asked, his eyes darkening.

"Stephen, do you love me for myself or do you love me because the children do?" Her heart stumbled as she gazed into his eyes.

His fingers tightened around her shoulders. "You're the reason I've hardly slept since we went to the cabin. You're the reason I've scarcely eaten. You're the reason my work has all but come to a stop. I don't need you as a nanny, Abby. I have Mrs. Bybee. I need you as a wife. Yes, I love you because the children do, but I love you for a thousand other reasons as well—your sassiness, your charm, those beautiful green eyes, your ability to make me feel whole again. I love the way you feel in my arms, the sound of your laughter, and the way you make my heart leap out of my chest at the sight of you. Is there anything else I can say to convince you that I love you?"

Abby touched her thumb to his bottom lip and shook her head. "I'm convinced."

He kissed her lightly. "If you're convinced, then say you'll marry me."

"Yes," she said, tears of joy forming in her eyes. "Tell

Daphne she will be getting a new mommy after all, as a belated gift for Christmas.''

He picked her up and swung her around. ''You've made me so happy.''

''Come,'' she said as her toes touched the ground. ''Let's tell Aunt Margo. She loves weddings.''

Hand in hand, they ran toward the ranch house with Ralphie nipping at their heels.